M000085290

THE MANUAL FOR
BRITISH MEN

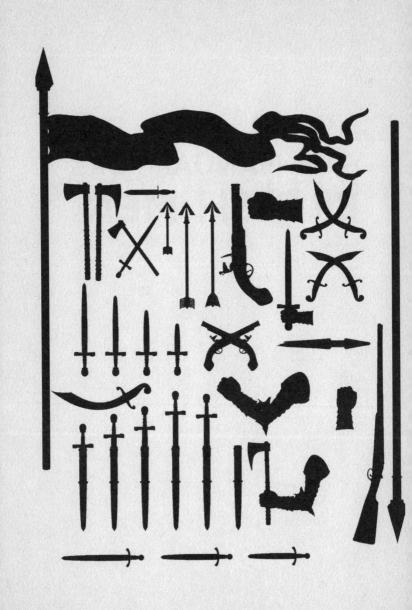

THE MANUAL FOR
BRITISH MEN

CHRIS MCNAB

The History Press

I dedicate this book to my father,
Brian McNab, who taught me the value of a good family,
dogged hard work and an inappropriate sense of humour.

All images are courtesy of
The History Press unless
otherwise indicated.

First published 2014

The History Press
The Mill, Brimscombe Port
Stroud, Gloucestershire, GL5 2QG
www.thehistorypress.co.uk

British Library Cataloguing in Publication Data.
A catalogue record for this book is available from the British Library.

ISBN 978 0 7509 5913 1

Typesetting and origination by The History Press
Printed in Great Britain

CONTENTS

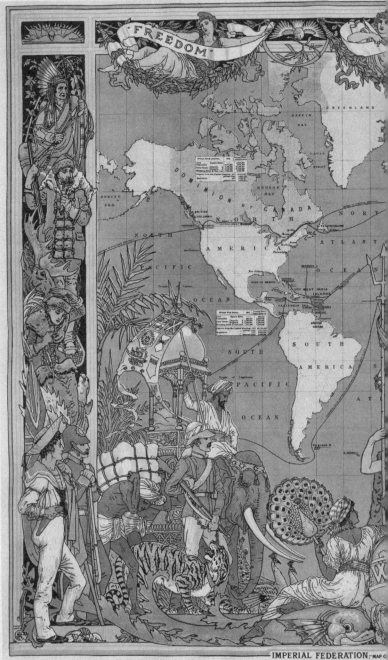

FREEDOM

IMPERIAL FEDERATION—MAP O

FEDERATION

MAP OF THE WORLD.
SHOWING THE EXTENT OF THE BRITISH TERRITORIES IN 1786.

THE BRITISH EMPIRE IN 1886.

MACLURE & CO QUEEN VICTORIA STREET LONDON.

Chapter I

Defender of
the Realm

HE LEAVES HIS HORSE AND TAKES
HIS WOUNDED FRIEND UPON HIS SHOULDERS
AND BEARS HIM PAST THE VALLEY OF
DEATH AND DANGER!

Section One
Blood and Steel

• FIRE A MUSKET •

Handling your 'Brown Bess' Land Pattern Musket well is often all that keeps you from death at the hands of some enraged heathen foe. To load and fire smartly, first take out a paper cartridge (containing powder and ball) and tear off the top with your teeth – don't worry, you'll quickly get a taste for cordite. Pull back the hammer to half cock, lift the frizzen and prime the pan (the metal hollow beneath the hammer) with a little powder; close the frizzen quickly to stop losing your powder to the wind or rain. Now stand Bess upright, and pour the rest of the powder down the barrel. You're left with a section of empty paper containing the musket ball. Musket ball first, drop this into the barrel, and use your ramrod to tap the whole lot down, tight as the drummer's snare skin. Now present your musket to the shoulder, pull back the hammer to full cock, and take aim. All being well, pulling the trigger will yield smoke, fire and one fewer enemy to worry about.

• Fire a cannon •

There's no standing on ceremony when firing a cannon – lively teamwork is of the essence. You are one of five numbered gunners – the No. 1 gun commander, of course. First step – your No. 2 spongeman uses his sponge to clear out any remnants from the previous shot, including those glowing embers that might prematurely detonate the next charge. The No. 3 loader now gets to business, inserting a charge of powder (contained in a paper bag) then a ball, which the No. 2 rams down using a 12ft-long rammer stick. While he is doing so, the No. 4 ventsman places his thumb over the vent hole at the rear – we don't want air rushing into the vent to fan any flames left alive in the barrel. The gun's getting lively now. The ventsman pushes a long needle down through the vent hole, puncturing the gunpowder bag and exposing the power. Now a slow match is inserted down through the vent hole. The moment has come. Death is levelled at the serried ranks at our front, the slow match is lit, and with a deafening 'crump', a cannonball splits air and men.

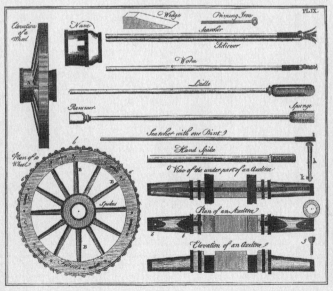

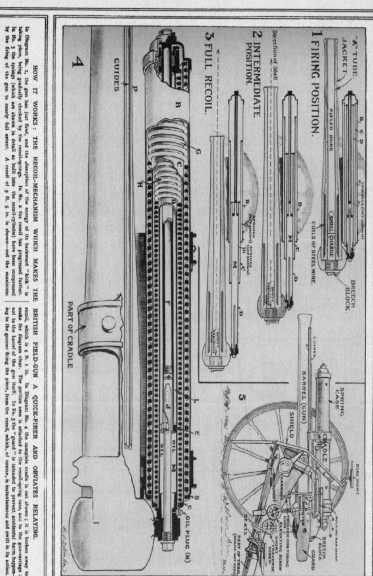

"A" TUBE.
JACKET.
B, C, D SPRINGS (NOT SHOWN)
PIFLED BORE
COILS OF STEEL WIRE
SHELL CHARGE
BREECH BLOCK

1 FIRING POSITION.

2 INTERMEDIATE POSITION.

Direction of Shell

3 FULL RECOIL.

GUIDES

4 PART OF CRADLE

5 DIAL SIGHT · BARREL (GUN) · SPRING CASE · SHIELD · CRADLE · GUIDES · SEATS · BREECH BLOCK · GUARD

OIL · OIL PLUG (K)

HOW IT WORKS: THE RECOIL-MECHANISM WHICH MAKES THE BRITISH FIELD-GUN A QUICK-FIRER AND OBVIATES RELATING.

In Diagram No. 1, the gun has just fired, and the absorption of the energy of its backward "kick" is taking place, being gradually checked by the recoil-springs. In No. 2 the recoil has progressed further. In No. 3 the springs (which are shown in detail as built into the recoil-cylinder) have been compressed by the firing of the gun to nearly full extent. A recoil of 3 ft. 5 in. is shown—not the maximum

recoil, which is 4 ft. 1 in. In Diagram No. 4 the complete cradle is not shown; it is broken away to make the diagram clear. The portion seen is attached to the recoil-spring case, and to the gun-carriage; not to the barrel of the gun itself. In No. 5 the "guard" is intended to prevent, accidental harm happening to the gunner firing the piece, from the recoil, which, of course, is instantaneous and swift in its action.

◆ WARRIOR ON A ROLL: JOHN CHURCHILL, ◆
1ST DUKE OF MARLBOROUGH (1650–1722)

The 1st Duke of Marlborough, John Churchill, is famous
for both his military genius and his famous descendants.
Churchill saw the rise and fall of five British monarchs
during his career (under whom he also rose and fell in favour
due to his shifting alliances), but his greatest supporter
would be Queen Anne, who was a close friend of his wife,
Sarah Jennings. Churchill secured great military victories
for his queen, most notably during the War of the Spanish
Succession (1701–14) – raise your glasses for his victories
at Blenheim (1704), Ramillies (1706), Oudenarde (1708),
and Malplaquet (1709). It was under his giant personality
that the Allied forces were honed into a united and
well-regarded army, developing the status and wealth of his
beloved Britain. What true Brit could ask for more?

• Use a longbow •

Scourge of the French at Agincourt (1415), the longbow –
at beween 5 and 6ft in length, and with a draw weight of up
to 185lb – is not a weapon for the weak. That's why you were
chosen – your powerful arms and shoulders and your barrel
chest make you an ideal archer. Anyway, no time to waste,
as the enemy is gathering. Raise up your bow, with stave in
the left hand and string in the right, body oriented toward the
enemy. Take an arrow, with either a bodkin head (for tackling
plate armour and mail) or broadhead (for deep penetration into
the body), and nock the rear of the arrow onto the bowstring;
the front shaft of the arrow is resting on the bow-hand knuckle.
Use three fingers to draw the string, the arrow resting between
forefinger and middle finger (keep the fingers spaced enough so
they aren't pinched between string and arrow
at full draw). Hold the bow low, then draw
by opening out the chest and shoulders
powerfully while raising the bow and
pulling back on the drawstring –
no trembling now, just one
smooth movement until the
thumb of the draw hand touches
your earlobe. Keep your eye on
the target at all times, and apply
the correct aim and elevation. Don't
hold this position for more than three
seconds, or muscle fatigue will weaken
aim and shot. Instead, release the string
cleanly, pushing back with your elbow
to sharpen the loose. Your arrow is now
in flight, delivering whistling death
over 400yds.

• DRESS A WARHORSE •

Your destrier won't be alive long on the medieval battlefield unless you apply the requisite barding (armour for horses). The face is protected by a plate armour *champron*, ideally with hinged cheek pieces. The *criniere* shields the neck, the *peytral* the chest, the *croupier* guards those muscular hind quarters (the horse will get decidedly frisky with an arrow in those) and the *flanchard* shields the flanks. Thus clad, your horse should be able to thunder through arrow, spear and sword. For appropriate grandeur, drape the entire armoured beast in a *caparison* (a long decorative cloth), and action beckons on thundering hooves. Both you, and the horse, may not live out the day, but at least you'll ride into death looking magnificent.

• FIGHT WITH A LONGSWORD •

The longsword is a brutish instrument, perfect for cleaving a Frenchman or Spaniard in two. But, at nearly 50in long, it takes mind and muscle to wield effectively. If facing an armoured opponent, don't slash with the edge of the blade at the enemy's armour plate – all you'll achieve is a blunt, dead sword. Instead, drive the point of the blade home into those soft, unprotected areas between the joints of the armour, such as the face, armpit and joint of the elbow. Assist the thrust, and make it more accurate, with a hand near the point of the blade – this is known as 'half swording' – and lean your body weight forward. You'll know that you've hit home when the blood flows, so be prepared to kick your victim off the blade and move on to the next.

• KILL A KNIGHT •

Just because you're a humble infantryman doesn't mean you can't take on one of those knights, gleaming in their armour on horseback. First, you might get the archers to nobble him at range – one of those bodkin head arrows, fired from a good longbow, can sometimes punch straight through armour into the knight's noble heart. If he gets through to your lines, however, work together with your mates. Drag him from the horse with the 'thorn' of your halberd (a long, two-handed pole weapon with fearsome blade and a snagging spike), and once he's on the floor, all cumbersome and struggling in the mud, thrust the point of your halberd straight into a soft part. On the other hand, get close and you can slip your stiletto knife between the joints of his armour, doing some nasty work inside. Either way, 200 years of martial family tradition isn't going to save him.

• SET A BOOBY TRAP FOR THE GERMANS •

Here's an easy way of repurposing ration tins and taking out a handful of Boche in one go. Fix two tin cans to two trees on opposite sides of a track. Keep the cans low, about jackboot height. Now take a standard Mills grenade and pull the pin – by all that's holy be careful: don't release that pin, whatever you do. Now push the grenade into one of the cans, so the pin is held in nicely by the metal wall. Do the same with the other can and another grenade. You're nearly there – string a thin wire between the bodies of the two grenades (rub the wire with a little dirt; you don't want its shine giving away your booby trap). Now leave well alone. The idea is that the German comes sauntering along, trips the wire which pulls the grenades from the cans, releasing the pins. Four seconds later – boom, job done.

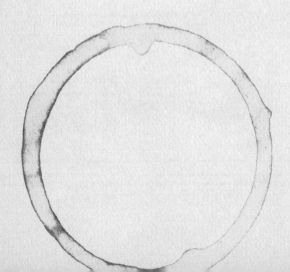

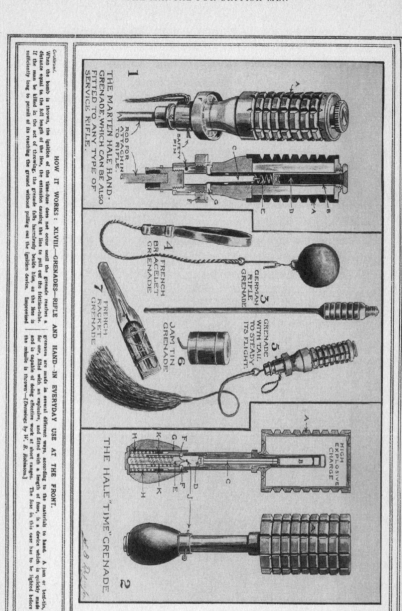

THE MARTEN HALE HAND-GRENADE, WHICH CAN BE ALSO FITTED TO ANY TYPE OF SERVICE RIFLE.

ROD FOR ATTACHING TO RIFLE.

SAFETY PIN

1

4 FRENCH BRACELET GRENADE

3 GERMAN RIFLE GRENADE

7 FRENCH RACKET GRENADE

6 JAM TIN GRENADE

5 GRENADE WITH TAIL TO STEADY ITS FLIGHT.

HIGH EXPLOSIVE CHARGE

THE HALE "TIME" GRENADE

2

Continued.

When the bomb is thrown, the ignition of the time-fuse does not occur until the grenade reaches a distance equal to the full length of the line, the detonation causing the line to pull out the friction-tube. If the man be killed in the act of throwing, the grenade thus harmlessly beside him, as the line is sufficiently long to permit of its reaching the ground without pulling out the ignition device. Improvised

HOW IT WORKS: XLVIII.—GRENADES—RIFLE AND HAND—IN EVERYDAY USE AT THE FRONT. grenades are made in several different ways, according to the materials to hand. A jam or best-tin, for one, filled with an explosive, and fitted with a length of fuse, is a device which is quickly made and is capable of doing effective work at short ranges. The fuse in this case has to be lighted before the missile is thrown.—[*Drawings by W. B. Robinson.*]

• FIGHT IN THE CELTIC BATTLE LINE •

To fight alongside the Celts against the Romans, cast aside your humanity. You're armed with all manner of hacking and smashing weapons – short sword, longsword, two-handed hammer, battle axe – and the only way you're going to use them is to get close enough to the enemy to feel his dying breath. (Make sure your sword is in singing condition – many Celtic blades are apt to snap or bend as soon as they strike something solid.) You're not armoured, so you can move fast, and you need the speed – the Roman line will be disciplined and well protected, so you have to overwhelm it in a frenzied attack referred to by the Romans as the 'the Furor Celtica' (Celtic fury). Cross the ground fast, close with the enemy ranks and go beserk, hacking and slashing at anything that moves or speaks funny. If the Romans surge back, or unleash their archers, form a robust shield wall and don't let them in. Hold firm, cut hard, and you'll win the day.

• Crush the Vikings •

They're merciless Norsemen from across the sea, but they can be defeated if you think with your head and fight with your arm. Take the Battle of Stamford Bridge (1066), the victory of King Harold Godwinson over Harald Hardrada, King of Norway (and Tostig, brother of King Harold, treacherously allied to the Vikings). The Vikings made mistakes – they split their army on both sides of the River Derwent, and left much of their armour on their ships. Those on the west side were annihilated by an English attack, but the English onslaught was slowed by having to cross a bridge to the east side. There the Vikings made a shield wall, but the English formed up, locked shields and charged. The battle raged for hours, and eventually English spirit (and outflanking manoeuvres) triumphed over Viking aggression. The Viking line broke, Hardrada and Tostig were slain, and the myth of Viking invincibility was sunk like a leaky longboat.

◆ EARLY BRITISH DEFENDER: HAROLD II *(c.* 1020–1066*)* ◆

The last Anglo-Saxon ruler of England, Harold II had earlier inherited the Earldom of East Anglia from his father, but had fallen into dispute with his brother, Tostig. Medieval warrior families weren't known for their loyalty, and Tostig joined forces with Harald Hardrada of Norway, who contested the English crown as well as William, Duke of Normandy. However, the handsome and courageous Harold was crowned King of England after the death of Edward the Confessor in January 1066. He would not have long to enjoy his reign, first facing Harald Hardrada and Tostig at Stamford Bridge near York in September 1066, before confronting William less than a month later at Hastings. The battle at Hastings was hard and close-matched as both sides struggled to gain the advantage, but the Normans under William the Conqueror finally took the field. The exact cause of Harold's death is unknown, but history prefers an arrow to the eye, as seen in the famous Bayeux Tapestry. After that, life would never be the same for Old England.

• FORM A SHIELD WALL •

The medieval shield wall requires strong nerves to form
and hold. It's ideal for an inexperienced militia army, who
are better at grunting, pushing and shoving than at nimble
swordplay. Your primary tools are a long kite shield and
a 6–8ft thrusting spear. Stand shoulder to shoulder with
your comrades on the front rank, your shields overlapping
to limit your exposure. Behind you will be another rank of
shield-and-sword men, giving you momentum, while behind
them are men armed with javelins, to throw when a glimpse
of exposed human being presents itself. Thus tightly packed,
you must crash forward onto the enemy ranks, shoving with
the shield and thrusting through the gaps with your spear.
Eventually, a combination of muscle and steel will wear down
one side or the other – make sure it's the enemy who collapses.

• Perform a Battlefield Amputation •

With the application of chloroform as an anaesthetic
(1847), battlefield amputations have become a breeze for
the indefatigable military surgeon. There's no slacking,
however – you are still expected to perform one every 10–15
minutes *in extremis*. First, send the patient off to dreamland
with a chloroform-soaked rag. Next strap a tourniquet
above the injury – make sure it's nice and tight, otherwise
your patient will bleed to death on the table once you start
cutting. Now to it – slice through all the skin and muscle,
right down to the bone. Switch to your bone saw, and work
quickly through the bone itself. The leg should now come free
(always surprisingly heavy). Tie the exposed blood vessels with
sutures, and stitch up the whole ghastly wound, although leave
a drainage hole in the stump. Throw the leg away – the poor
fellow's not going to need it again. Strangely, some one in four
amputees will die after the operation. Might be something to
do with a lack of sterilisation, but only history will tell …

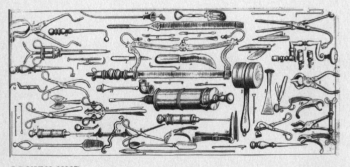

(LC-USZ62-62067)

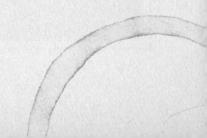

• LAUNCH A CAVALRY CHARGE •

Nothing beats the sheer bloody exhilaration of the cavalry charge. The trick is to race together in one thundering mass, to generate momentum and a combined force that will smash through the enemy ranks, throwing them into disorder and rout. Therefore you need to follow the pace commands: 'Attention for the charge!' ... 'Forward, walk march!' ... 'Trot' ... 'Canter' ... 'Gallop!' ... 'Charge!' The gallop and charge take place only for the last hundred yards or so, by which time you'll have also received the order to draw your swords. When you hit the enemy ranks, slash downwards with your sabre, aiming for the skull, neck and shoulders. If you have a couched lance, lean well forward and take your weight firmly in the stirrups – hit a fellow with this at 40mph and you're liable to be lifted out the saddle if everything's not solid. Once you've broken the enemy ranks, the field may well be yours. You can then spend a jaunty afternoon hunting down the stragglers, fleeing like rabbits across the field.

• RESIST A CAVALRY CHARGE •

The eighteenth-century cavalry charge might strike fear into the hearts of the weak, but with some stout tactics and resilient attitude, you'll survive the day. Make sure that you hold your ranks tightly, either in square or line, but strengthen the flanks to avoid the cavalry outflanking you. Inflict casualties on the charging enemy with musket and cannon even before they reach you – even the mightiest warhorse will be brought down in ghoulish fashion by grapeshot and ball. Present bayonets to the front in a solid, glittering wall; the riders will likely slow when they get close (sometimes to discharge handguns or carbines), as crashing into your blades is good for neither horse nor cavalryman. If the horse does break through your lines, try to dispatch it either with musket shot or bayonet thrust to the neck or abdomen, or a sword swipe to the leg. Watch it though – if you are in closely packed ranks the enemy's artillery is likely to send cannonballs into your midst. Nothing says 'mortality' like a man's brains all over your tunic.

◆ THE IRON DUKE: WELLINGTON (1769–1852) ◆

Lauded for his decisive defeat of Napoleon during the Battle of Waterloo in 1815, the Duke of Wellington participated in approximately sixty battles during his impressive military career (not bad for a man who only joined the army to please his mother!). It was at Waterloo that Wellington and his men proved their mettle, forcing the French to retreat and finally bring about the abdication of Napoleon. (Apparently the Prussians also had some part to play in the action …) Later becoming British Prime Minister, Wellington led his beloved country from 1828–30, and again in 1834. As PM, Wellington was rather less competent. However, the Great Duke remains popular as a fearless warrior and an incorruptible leader of men who always remained human enough to weep for those lost in battle. He is also credited for inventing the Wellington boot, most useful when tramping across one's country estate.

• FIGHT WITH A PIKE •

The Renaissance pike is a king of weapons. Anywhere up to 25ft long, made of strong wood such as ash (to stop it flexing too much) and with a vicious spearhead at the end, it's changed the military landscape. Tactically, it's best used in close-packed, ordered linear ranks. In battle, the frontal ranks hold the pikes out at 'charge', bristling towards the enemy and ready to deliver thrusts. For defending against horses, the heavy brutes, the rear of the pike could be stuck in the ground and spear angled upwards, known as 'charge for horse' – even an 18-hand warhorse will skewer itself proper on that. Those further back will raise their pikes at 'port', angled safely above the heads of those in front. In cases where the enemy is attempting to surround you, a 'pike square' or hedgehog-like formation will provide decent defence. Don't rely on your pike too much, however. At close quarters they are as useless as a trimmed sapling, so have that sword, mace or dagger at the ready in case you have to slug it out man to man.

• DRESS LIKE A KNIGHT •

You've spent a crippling fortune on a suit of plate armour, now it's just a question of putting it on. When dressing for battle, helped by your obsequious squire, first put on your 'arming doublet', a thick quilted jacket to protect your flesh from the mail coat of up to 20,000 rings, which you wear on top. Now work from the feet upwards. The *sabaton*, *greave*, *poleyn* and *cuisse* protect the feet, shins, knees and thighs respectively. *Tassets* shield the upper legs while your chest is guarded by the breastplate. A multitude of different pieces wrap around your hands (here specifically the infamous gauntlets, thrown at the feet of many a contender), arms and shoulders, while the *gorget* encases that ever-vulnerable neck. The helmet takes care of your skull and face, but visibility is poor (make sure all the ventilation slits are clear). All told, it will take you about fifteen minutes to don your armour. When the arrows and blades start pinging off the plate, you'll thank God for every pound and shilling spent.

(LC-USZ62-17351)

Section Two
Britain Needs You!

• FIRE A VICKERS MACHINE GUN •

Firing the Vickers machine gun is a godlike experience, no doubt. There's nothing more enlivening to body and mind than sending .303in rounds, each with a killing range of well over a mile (up to 4,500 yards for indirect plunging fire), across no-man's-land at 500rpm. She's a robust girl (ten guns of the 100th Company of the Machine Gun Corps, in August 1915, fired more than one million rounds continuously over a period of twelve hours), but needs good handling. To fire: once the tripod is set up and the gun mounted, fill the barrel jacket with water. (*In extremis*, when the gun is running hot and boiling away the fluid, you can add urine.) Using the port near the muzzle, connect the jacket to a condenser can via the supplied hose. Now, let's give her some teeth. Insert the end strip of the canvas ammo belt into the feed chute, and pull through from the other side until it stops. Cock the gun twice with the handle on the right side of the receiver. She's just about ready to roar. Set your rear ladder sight for range, then grip the firing handles. Pull in the safety levers, then push in the spade trigger. Like a fire-spitting Rolls-Royce, the gun will burst into life. The Hun had better keep his head down …

PULL WHICH WILL RAISE WHEELS
SAFE PULL TO APPLY (TOTAL, 1, 2 AND 3)
1. RESISTANCE OF OIL IN CYLINDER
2. RESISTANCE OF SPRINGS
3. RESISTANCE OF FRICTION

HOW IT WORKS: THE MODERN FIELD-GUN EMPLOYED IN THE WAR—ITS RECOIL-MECHANISM EXPLAINED.

[Continued.]

The arrangement seen at E is typical of most spring-return carriages. At F is the cross-section of the piston and the cylinder which has longitudinal ribs on its interior; also an enlarged section of one of the ribs along which the slots in the piston move in recoil, gradually closing the parts until the end of recoil. The relationship between the parts will be understood by noting the details of the gun-carriage at D. (1) Sheet-steel cradle containing recoil-cylinder and springs; (2) Clips under the gun, sliding on guides on the cradle; (3) Rear end of recoil-cylinder; (4) Nut attaching recoil-cylinder to lug on gun; (5) Sight for direction; (6) Quadrant for elevation. B shows a gun firing; note the instantaneous recoil.—[Letterpress and Diagrams Reproduced by Courtesy of the "Scientific American."]

• DIG A FRONTLINE TRENCH •

Your back will almost certainly break when digging a frontline trench. At least you'll have company – about 450 men can dig a 250yd trench section in around six hours. The basic trench is about 7ft deep and 6ft wide, with the enemy-facing lip known as the parapet, and the opposite lip known as the parados. Both are reinforced with thick layers of sandbags to protect the occupants from shell splinters and bullets. The parados is also, ideally, higher than the parapet, so the trench occupants aren't silhouetted against the sky. A wooden or earth fire-step, 2–3ft high, is cut into the front wall of the trench, for a soldier to stand on to see through or over the parapet, and dugouts carved into the walls of the trench basically serve as wormy accommodation, typically roofed with corrugated iron or wood. Duckboards line the bottom of the trench, to help keep your feet out of the mud and water that collect there like soggy sponge pudding. To make the whole trench solid, support the walls with sandbags, wooden revetting and wire mesh. Don't expect luxury, but the trench will feel like home when the shells start falling …

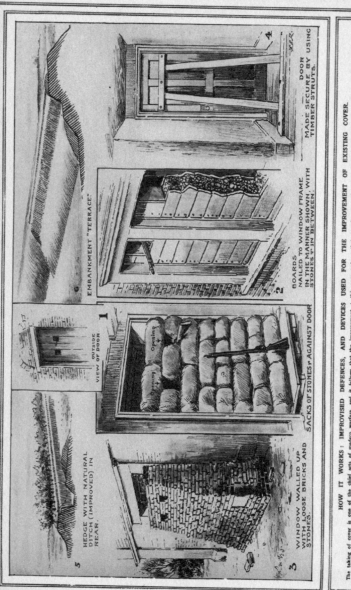

HEDGE WITH NATURAL DITCH (IMPROVED) IN REAR.

WINDOW WALLED UP WITH LOOSE BRICKS AND STONES.

SACKS OF STONES & AGAINST DOOR

OUTSIDE VIEW OF DOOR

EMBANKMENT "TERRACE."

BOARDS NAILED TO WINDOW FRAME IN THE MANNER SHOWN, WITH STONES V. IN BETWEEN.

DOOR MADE SECURE BY USING TIMBER STRUTS.

HOW IT WORKS: IMPROVISED DEFENCES, AND DEVICES USED FOR THE IMPROVEMENT OF EXISTING COVER.

The taking of cover is one of the chief arts of modern warfare, and it follows that the improvement of existing defences, natural or artificial, is a matter of equal importance in the operations of troops. The nature of such defences, of course, varies to an almost unlimited extent according to the character of the locality and the kind of materials available for constructing them. Our artist has illustrated on this page and on that opposite a number of typical methods by which houses, walls, hedges, embankments, and so on, can be put into a stronger state of defence for the use of infantry. The different devices illustrated in the drawings are explained in the article on the opposite page. Sand-bags, or sacks filled with earth or stones, have been largely used during the war.—[Drawn by W. B. Robinson.]

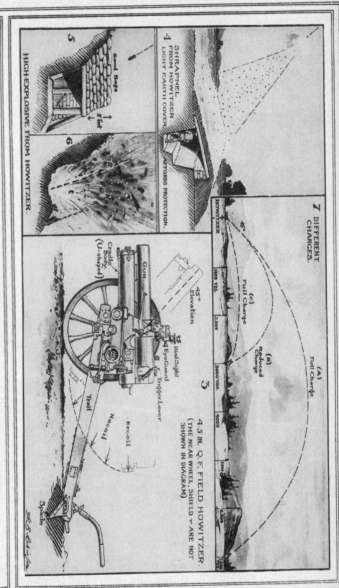

HOW IT WORKS : A HOWITZER IN DIAGRAM, TO SHOW ITS GENERAL MECHANISM AND RANGES.

4.5 IN. Q.F. FIELD HOWITZER.
(THE NEAR WHEEL, SHIELD v ARE NOT SHOWN IN DIAGRAM.)

7 DIFFERENT CHARGES.

SHRAPNEL FROM HOWITZER FROM LIGHT EARTH COVER AFFORDS PROTECTION.

HIGH-EXPLOSIVE FROM HOWITZER.

(Continued.)

Howitzers are also used to break in overhead-cover with high-explosives, as seen in Figs. 5 and 6. Earth head-cover will keep out howitzer shrapnel-bullets, but howitzer high-explosive shells will go through the roof of a shelter covered with five feet of sand-bags and burst inside the shelter, totally demolishing it and killing all within. In Fig. 7, (A) represents a howitzer firing a full charge with 45 deg. elevation to 7000 yards' range. (B) shows the trajectory at 9000 yards with the full charge and reduced elevation. (C) shows, at 1000 yards, with the full charge and reduced elevation. For the various ranges at which howitzers may be required to operate, special charges are supplied on service for each weapon, each howitzer, in fact, being supplied with no fewer than seven sizes of cartridge.

• RAID AN ENEMY TRENCH •

You can't be squeamish when choosing your weapons for a
trench raid. Spiked clubs, daggers, sharpened entrenching
tools, hatchets, brass knuckles, handguns, plenty of grenades –
anything you can use to best the Boche in a tight space should
be taken. You're going to be working at night and in a small
team, often grouped into four: two riflemen and two bomb
throwers (armed with grenades). Work carefully and quietly
across no-man's-land and under the wire – any indiscipline
with noise or light is likely to bring the hammers of death down
upon you – then jump into the trench and get stuck in with your
knives or clubs. If your job, as rifleman, is then to clear a section
of trench, let the bomb thrower clear each bay and dugout
first with a grenade before you whip around the corner with
handgun and spiked club to finish the job. Once you've alerted
the enemy, however, they are going to open up with everything
they've got. Good luck in getting back …

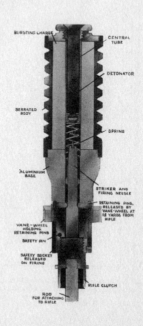

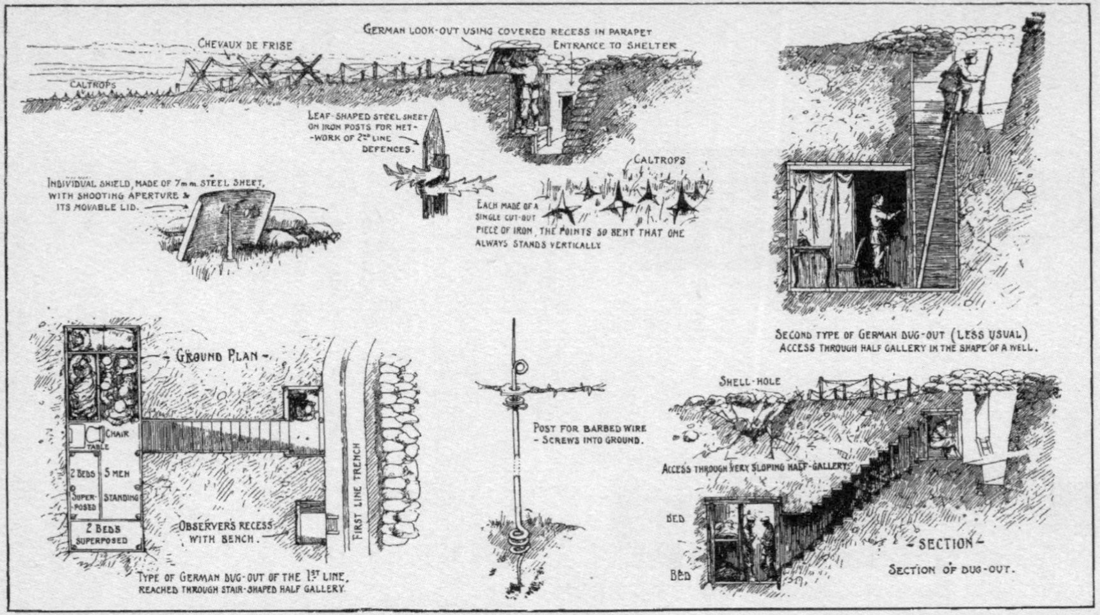

WHAT THE BRITISH AND FRENCH TROOPS HAD TO ATTACK IN THEIR VICTORIOUS ADVANCE: DEEP AND SOLID GERMAN TRENCH-WORKS.

The heroism of the French and British troops in their recent victories can only be appreciated when it is remembered what formidable defence works they had to attack. These drawings show typical examples of German trenches, dug-out shelters, and accessory defences. The most remarkable feature is the extraordinary depth of the officers' dug-outs, often twenty-five or thirty feet beneath the surface, and reached either by steps down a sloping gallery, or by a ladder in a vertical shaft. Outside the trenches are barbed-wire entanglements, *chevaux-de-frise*, saw-edged fencing, and four-pointed caltrops, so made that one point always sticks up when they are thrown on the ground. The lower diagrams right and left are a sectional view and a ground-plan of the same dug-out.—[*By Courtesy of* "*L'Illustration.*"]

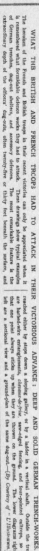

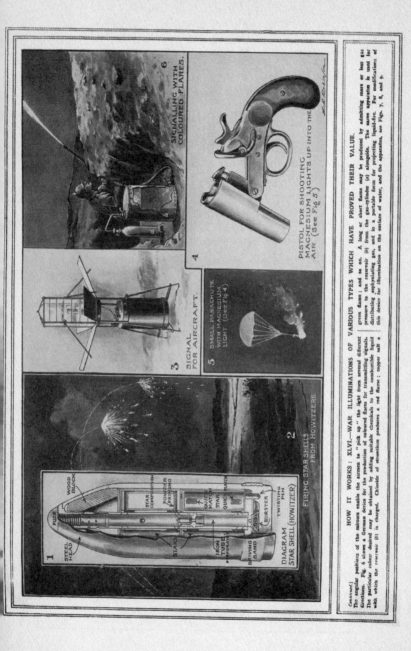

HOW IT WORKS: XLVI—WAR ILLUMINATIONS OF VARIOUS TYPES WHICH HAVE PROVED THEIR VALUE.

Continued.]
The angular positions of the mirrors enable the airman to "pick up" the light from several different directions. Fig. 6 shows a German device for producing coloured flares for transmitting signals. The particular colour desired may be obtained by adding suitable chemicals to the combustible liquid with which the reservoir (b) is charged. Chloride of strontium produces a red flame; copper salt a green flame; and so on. A long or short flame may be produced by admitting more or less gas pressure to the reservoir (b) from the gas-cylinder (a) alongside. The same apparatus is used for distributing asphyxiating gas, and in a portable form for projecting liquid-fire. For modification of this device for illumination on the surface of water, and the adaptation of the apparatus, see Figs. 7, 8, and 9.

1 DIAGRAM STAR SHELL (HOWITZER)

STEEL HEAD
FUZE
WOOD BLOCK
STAR COMPOSITION
POWDER PRIMING
QUICK MATCH
STAR
QUICK MATCH
BURSTER
TWISTING PIN
IRON TUBE PERFORATED
STARS
DRIVING BAND

2 FIRING STAR SHELLS FROM HOWITZERS

3 SIGNAL FOR AIRCRAFT.

4 PISTOL FOR SHOOTING MAGNESIUM LIGHTS UP INTO THE AIR. (See Fig. 5)

5 SMALL PARACHUTE WITH MAGNESIUM LIGHT. (See Fig. 4)

6 SIGNALLING WITH COLOURED FLARES.

• Snipe across no-man's-land •

To be an effective sniper, you need more self-control than the average man. Most of your time will be taken up observing, scanning the landscape for those tiny signs of movement that indicate a human target. Your rifle – a .303in Lee-Enfield or even a good hunting rifle – should be in excellent condition with properly ranged sights, and equipped with the best-quality ammunition you can find (no nicks or scratches on the bullet head).

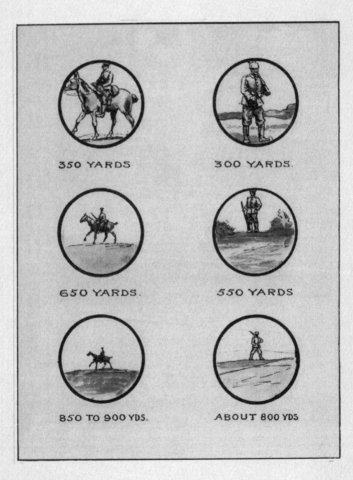

350 YARDS   300 YARDS.

650 YARDS.   550 YARDS

850 TO 900 YDS.   ABOUT 800 YDS

Rest the fore-end on a stable platform, such as a pile of earth or a sandbag. You've spotted the target, blithely tucking into his rations and unaware of the gun-sight levelled at his head. Estimate range and adjust your sights (optical or iron) for windage and elevation. Control your breathing to reduce muscular tension (which causes shake in the gun) – a slow exhalation, deep in-breath, then half exhalation and hold. In this still moment, with the clueless enemy living out his last few moments munching on poor-quality sausage, steady your aim and squeeze the trigger.

(*Illustrated War News*, August 1915)

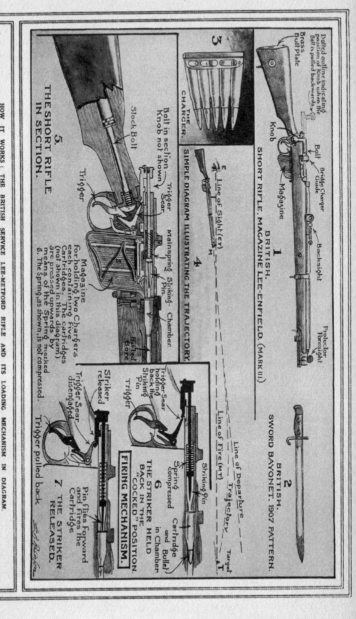

HOW IT WORKS : THE BRITISH SERVICE LEE-METFORD RIFLE AND ITS LOADING MECHANISM IN DIAGRAM.

[Comment]

Pressure on the trigger disengages the trigger-sear, releasing the firing-pin, which flies forward, under the influence of the mainspring, and fires the cartridge (Fig. 7). To reload, the bolt is pulled back as before described, the extractor situated in its forward-end withdrawing the discharged case, which is then thrown from the breech, and its place taken by the next cartridge in the magazine. When the target is moving, allowance must be made for this. A man walking across the line of fire will be hit if aim be taken one foot in front of him for every hundred yards in the distance between the man and the rifle. A man moving at the double requires two feet allowance, a trotting horse, three feet, and a horse passing at a gallop, four feet.

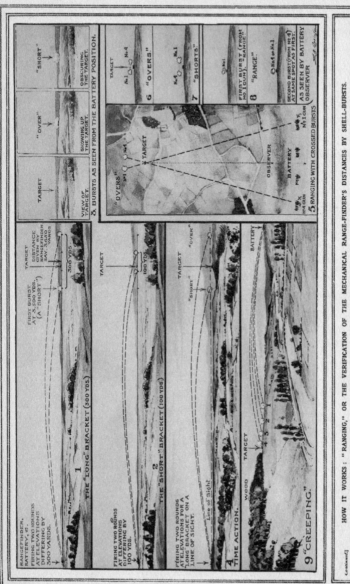

HOW IT WORKS: "RANGING," OR THE VERIFICATION OF THE MECHANICAL RANGE-FINDER'S DISTANCES BY SHELL-BURSTS.

• AVOID THE SNIPERS •

I tend to place a high value on the integrity of my skull. If you do too, listen up, for here are my top sniper-survival tips for trench life. First, and most obvious, keep your head well below the parapet at all times. This is particularly the case when walking past low sections of trench – Jerry will have his rifle already pre-zeroed on this location, and all he needs is a second of Mk1 Brodie helmet to appear to show you the gates of heaven. (These sections should be marked with a board warning everyone to duck low and stay low.) Second, lighting up your fag at night can invite a 7.92mm fate. Never light more than three cigarettes from one match at the same time – the first light alerts the sniper, the second allows him to take aim, and the third gives him the shot. Finally, if you have to take a peak over the parapet, use a trench mirror to do the viewing – a sneaky peak with the naked eye might simply have you staring down the barrel of a Mauser.

• MAKE A BAYONET CHARGE •

You've spent hours refining your bayonet fighting technique – Left parry! Right parry! Forward lunge! – but rarely seem to put it into practice. No surprise there – guns and artillery have made the bayonet largely obsolete (although not for opening tin cans). Nevertheless, take every opportunity you can to present cold steel (17in of the Pattern 1907 sword bayonet) to the enemy, especially if he's in the retreat. Scream your lungs out as you charge – show the Boche who's boss. If you catch him, thrust the bayonet at the soft parts – stomach, groin or (more difficult) throat – and use a quarter twist to extract. Don't go for the rib cage, as the blade will either bounce off or get stuck. When the blood flows or spurts, you'll feel every ounce the warrior, or sick to the stomach.

• DISPOSE OF THE DEAD •

Save your tears till later. Sometimes you have to bury the dead where they fall. Simply put their personal belongings into the gas helmet satchel (to return to relatives), dig a deep hole, place the body in the bottom and mark the grave with an identifier (cross, helmet etc.). Make sure you take with you the green vulcanised asbestos identity disk, leaving the red counterpart with the body. If opportunity presents itself to take the body out of the line and bury to the rear, chances are it will be transported in the same General Service wagons that brought up the rations (we didn't say war was hygienic). At the burial site (often consisting of large mass graves, located near Casualty Clearing Stations), wrap the body in hessian or simply a blanket, lay it in the grave, and say your goodbyes. A telegram will soon be winging its way to the next of kin in Blighty.

• AVOID TRENCH FOOT •

Trench foot is no fun, I can tell you. It's actually a stinking
fungal infection caused by long exposure to damp, insanitary
conditions – it's not a sign of malingering, as some of the
misinformed would have you. In fact, 20,000 of us went down
with the condition in 1914, and some lost toes to the blight.
The key to avoiding it is – stay dry. Change your socks regularly,
and put some grease on your toes to ward off the worst of the
damp. Make sure your trench has good duckboards on the floor
to keep you out of the water as much as possible. Your NCOs
should also conduct regular foot inspections, to see if you have
the early symptoms (numbness, red or blue colouration, blisters
and sores), or you might be paired with a comrade, and you're
both responsible for each other's feet. It ain't pretty … but you'll
do it for your mates.

• TUNNEL UNDER ENEMY TRENCHES •

As a member of the Royal Engineer tunnelling companies, life is dark, damp and dangerous. Like a mole in a tin hat, your job is to dig a deep tunnel under the opposing trenches, pack the end with explosives, then retreat to a safe distance and blow the enemy to kingdom come. If only life were so simple. You're working mostly by candlelight – not great if you have a build-up of explosive gas in the tunnel. Carbon monoxide can also render you unconscious or dead, which is why one of you carries a mouse or small bird in a cage – as soon as it passes out, get out. You usually work in 'clay kicking' teams of three: one to dig, one to fill sandbags and the other to take the sandbags out on a small trolley. Your day lasts up to twelve hours in cramped conditions, the dangers including premature detonation of explosives, tunnel collapse (the roof was shored up with wood) and even digging into an enemy tunnel. If the latter happens, you've got a fight on your hands. All being well, however, you might eventually create some of the biggest explosions on the battlefield, and leave a decent crater for tourists to photograph in years to come.

• LAY A MINEFIELD •

If you're laying a minefield, remember it's not just about blowing up the enemy. Place a minefield carefully, and it also controls how the enemy moves – by avoiding your minefield, he might channel himself onto your machine guns and artillery. A mixed field of anti-personnel and anti-tank mines covers just about all eventualities – stagger the placement of the mine rows so that any straight line of movement across the battlefield will result in a hit. You can frustrate the efforts of enemy sappers in trying to clear your mines by booby trapping individual mines with pressure-release or pull-firing devices, attached to a separate charge. Alternatively, you might want to be extra devious and link a few mines together with det-cord, resulting in multiple detonations for a single unfortunate step. Make your minefield work for you, but just don't forget where it is … it ain't going to feel so useful if you have to cross it.

TOP FIVE CAUSES OF DEATH IN
the SECOND WORLD WAR

Artillery – Here's a real killer. If we include mortars and grenades in this category, then the majority of all battlefield casualties in this conflict were caused by artillery.

Air-dropped bombs – Air power wiped out entire cities in the Second World War, as civilians were deliberately targeted. Bombs and artillery together accounted for around 70 per cent of all the war's casualties.

Bullet – There were billions of these things fired during the conflict, so naturally many found their mark. Surprisingly, however, they only account for around 10 per cent of casualties.

Mines – Anti-tank and anti-personnel mines, those traps for the unwary, take another 10 per cent of casualties.

Other – War's a dangerous business, and thousands of men died from a variety of other causes, including 'crushing' (according to one British Army report), 'chemical' (the same report, but vague on the details) and through the inevitable accidents which occur when you give hundreds of thousands of men weapons.

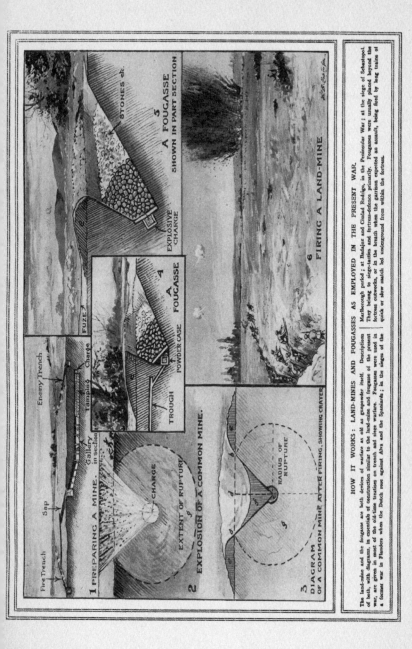

FIre Trench

Sap

Enemy Trench

Gallery
in section

Tamping

Charge

FUZE

1 PREPARING A MINE.

A FOUGASSE
SHOWN IN PART SECTION

STONES etc.

EXPLOSIVE
CHARGE

TROUGH

POWDER CASE

A
FOUGASSE

CHARGE

EXTENT OF RUPTURE

2 EXPLOSION OF A COMMON MINE.

RADIUS OF
RUPTURE

DIAGRAM
OF A COMMON MINE AFTER FIRING, SHOWING CRATER

3

6 FIRING A LAND-MINE

HOW IT WORKS: LAND-MINES AND FOUGASSES AS EMPLOYED IN THE PRESENT WAR.

The land-mines and the fougasse are both devices of warfare as old as gunpowder itself. Descriptions of both, with diagrams, in essentials of construction similar to the land-mine and fougasse of the present war, are given in most of the old-time treatises on trench and siege warfare. Fougasses were used in a former war in Flanders when the Dutch rose against Alva and the Spaniards; in the sieges of the Marlborough period; at Badajoz and Ciudad Rodrigo, in the Peninsular War; at the siege of Sebastopol. They belong to siege-tactics and fortress-defence primarily. Fougasses were usually placed beyond the fortress outworks, or in the breach when the garrison expected an assault, being fired by long trains of quick or slow match led underground from within the fortress.

• STRIP A BREN GUN •

To strip a Bren Gun for basic cleaning: 1: Take off the magazine; 2: Lift up the barrel nut catch; 3: Raise the carrying handle and remove the barrel; 4: Rotate and remove the bipod; 5: Push retainer pin flush with the regulator with the base of a round, turn gas regulator/bolt group and remove. Once the gun is stripped, remove any dirt or debris, then lightly oil any moving parts. (Don't use too much oil, or it will attract dust and turn into an abrasive grinding paste.) Pull through the barrel with solvent-soaked wads to remove propellant residue. Give everything a nice polish, then reassemble. Some soldiers on leave have trained their wives to do this job; it's not as if they have much else to do with their time, in between the full-time factory work, cooking, cleaning and looking after the kids.

• DRIVE A CHURCHILL TANK •

To drive 38 tons of boxy battletank, listen up. First, get the wireless operator to turn on the master switch in the battery compartment. Turn on the petrol pump and prime the carburettors and engine (using the petrol priming control and Ki-gass pump at the rear of the fighting compartment). Now press the ignition switch and starter button – you should hear the engine roar into life. To find a gear, press the clutch pedal and listen for the compressor dying down; just before it stops, ram the gear home. When changing gears during movement move the lever quickly and lightly, and don't press down too hard on the clutch stop with the pedal. Steering is via a servo-assisted tiller bar, and the Merritt-Brown gearbox allows you to steer by changing the relative speed of the two tracks. Don't get too excited – maximum speed is just 15mph.

Section Three
Blue-Sky Warrior – Air Warfare

• LAND A BIPLANE •

When landing your bullet-riddled and draughty Sopwith
Camel, you need intuition as much as skill if you are to avoid
death in tangled struts and blazing fuel. First, pick your landing
spot – an airfield is best, but any flat field will do, as long as
it's in the hands of our fellas. Start killing the speed on the
approach – drop down to about 65mph (no slower or you risk
a stall). Keep making minor corrections with the stick as you
flatten down towards the field, and your wings should be level
with the horizon. As you get close to the ground, start killing
off the power, and allow a gentle stall to drop your wheels
onto the grass. Expect some thumps and bumps – the Camel
can bounce a little more than other aircraft. Allow yourself
to settle, then taxi with insouciance over to the waiting
ground crew. A good breakfast is now the order of the day;
don't worry about putting on weight, as your life expectancy
is about five weeks.

(LC-USZC4-11182)

• DOGFIGHT IN A SPITFIRE •

The Spitfire's a good craft, but never underestimate Jerry in his Bf 109E. True, the Spit is about 12mph faster than the Bf 109 and its Merlin engine develops more power than the DB 601, but the Bf 109's 20mm cannon has more knock-down power than our .303 Browning machine guns. If you go up against a Bf 109, use all the Spit's advantages in manoeuvrability. If the Bf 109 is on your tail, build up as much speed as possible and get down to relatively low altitude, then perform a flick roll and dive. Hope that Jerry follows you. You can pull the Spit out of the dive sharpish, but the Messerschmitt's elevators are heavy at speed, and if you can't turn into a good shooting position then he might actually fly himself straight into the ground. That's one to brag about in the mess …

(LC-DIG-fsa-8b08065)

• USE A BOUNCING BOMB •

You've got 3 tons of Torpex explosive strapped into a 4-ton rotating bomb under your Lancaster, so obviously this is no ordinary mission. You're here to bust the Möhne Dam in the German Ruhr, and you're going to do so with Barnes Wallis' bouncing bomb. Ten minutes out from the target, you set the bomb rotating backwards at 500rpm in its drop cradle; the rotation will cause it to both stabilise and bounce when dropped onto the water. To ensure the bomb skips lively across the water, over the torpedo nets and strikes the dam, you have to drop it at exactly the right moment and speed – 230mph speed, 60ft altitude (you'll know you're at this height when the two intersecting searchlights underneath your aircraft form a figure of eight on the water) and 389m from the dam (calculated by triangulating between the dam's two towers). Oh, and you have to do this through hails of flak. Anyway, that's exactly what you do on the night of 16–17 May 1943, breaching the dam (your mates take care of the Edersee Dam), flooding the Ruhr valley and killing 1,600 people.

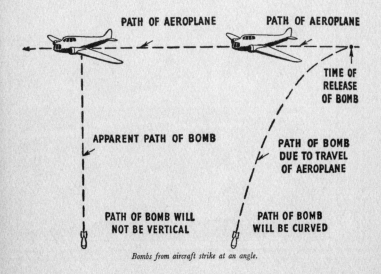

Bombs from aircraft strike at an angle.

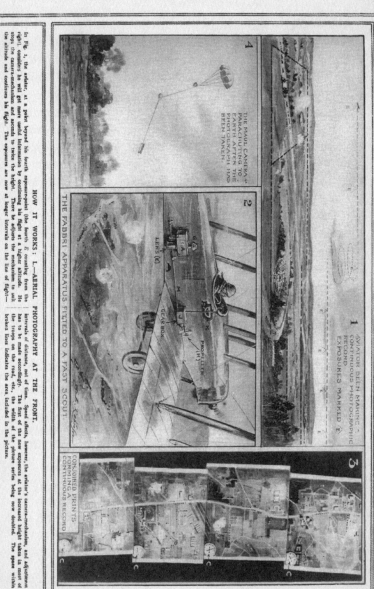

HOW IT WORKS : L.—AERIAL PHOTOGRAPHY AT THE FRONT.

THE MAUL CAMERA PARACHUTING TO EARTH AFTER THE PHOTOGRAPH HAS BEEN TAKEN.

AVIATOR SEEN MAKING A CONTINUOUS PHOTOGRAPHIC RECORD EXPOSURES MARKED 'F'

THE FABBRI APPARATUS FITTED TO A FAST SCOUT

LENS (C) — GEAR BOX — PROPELLER (F)

CONJOINED PRINTS FORMING A CONTINUOUS RECORD

In Fig. 1, the aviator, at a point beyond his fourth exposure-point (the fourth F counting from the right), considers he will get more until information by continuing his flight at a higher altitude. He stops the camera-mechanism and ascends to twice the height. There he adjusts the mechanism to suit the altitude and continues his flight. The exposures are now at longer intervals on the line of flight— intervals of distance, not of time. Speed affects, however, the aviator's camera-mechanism, and adjustment has to be made accordingly. The first of the new exposures at the increased height takes in most of the width of the picture series being now doubled. The space within the troops on the road, etc., the width of the picture series being now doubled. The space within broken lines indicates the area included in the picture.

• Strafe a Panzer in a Typhoon •

Flying your Typhoon as part of a 'cab rank' of ground-attack aircraft on the edge of the Normandy battlefield, 1944, it's natural that you are eager for a kill. The call comes in from the Forward Air Controller (FAC) on the ground – a German Tiger tank has been spotted loitering on the edge of woodland near the frontline, and could mess with our Shermans. You're given the coordinates and a description, and you fly in low, hugging the terrain to avoid enemy anti-aircraft fire. You identify the Tiger, and roar in at a speed of more than 400mph. You're spotted – a nearby German half-track crew opens up with an MG 42 on an AA mount, tracers zipping past your cockpit. It's too late, however. You fire off two of your eight RP-3 air-to-ground rockets, then give a half-second blast from your four 20mm Hispano cannon. Half-track and Tiger are wrecked in seconds, after which it's back to cab rank to wait for another customer.

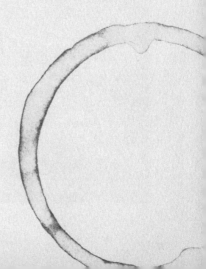

• ESCAPE A BURNING AIRCRAFT •

It's a hot night over Schweinfurt in 1944, and your Lancaster's starboard wing is on fire after an attack by Jerry night-fighters. What do you do? Well, Sergeant Norman Cyril Jackson RAFVR, 106 Squadron, has an answer. Simple – take one fire extinguisher, then climb out of the aircraft's escape hatch and onto the wing, while the crew hang onto your opened parachute. Oh, don't forget that you are already wounded with shell splinters. Try (unsuccessfully) to put out the fire, fall off the wing and get dragged underneath, eventually parachute down into German hands (badly burned and breaking your ankle on landing), spending the rest of the war in a POW camp. Receive the Victoria Cross after the war – but only when the other surviving crew members tell your story. Have you got all that? Off you go!

How it's done: making a Victoria Cross.

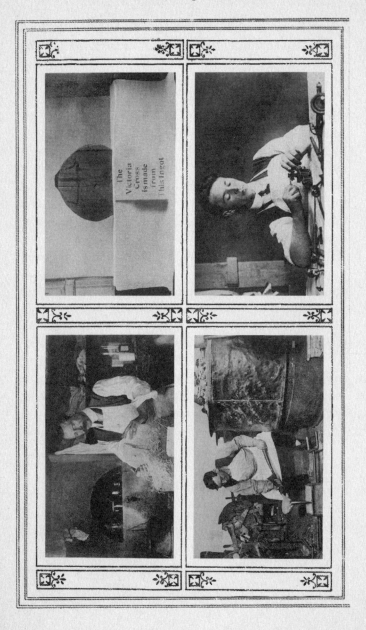

• SURVIVE BEING SHOT DOWN BEHIND ENEMY LINES •

You've been downed over occupied France. Although you have a fondness for French wine and some varieties of their cheese, you have no intention of a: becoming a French citizen; b: being taken prisoner by the Germans. Your first step home is to find out exactly where you are. Use your silk escape maps (one of your local area and one of the wider region) and your pocket compass for this; the silk maps can double up as bandages and ropes if need be. Your escape tin also includes some fishing hook and line, some unappetising but nutritious confectionary, a morphine injection and sulfanilamide tablets (to fight infections, if you have an open wound). Now, with care, make contact with the local resistance. You can communicate using either your public-school French (which seems to raise smirks amongst the locals) or the translation cards you might have been given. Approach someone in a remote location, and trust to their good nature. Once you are in resistance hands, clad yourself like a civilian (the tops of your flying boots are designed to be cut away to leave a rather unfashionable pair of shoes) then allow them to move you progressively between safe locations. You'll likely be using one of three major escape lines, two (codenamed 'Pat' and 'Comet') down to Spain, or one ('Shelburne') to southern England. It's going to be a gruelling journey, so chin up and keep thinking of that cold beer waiting for you in the Crown and Anchor.

• Man a Lancaster rear gun turret •

You've drawn a vital but short straw with your new job – tail gunner on a Lancaster bomber. You'll be lucky to survive more than four missions (most of the German night-fighter attacks take place from the rear), but some men do, so take heart. The worst part of the job can be the isolation – stuck at the back in an FN-120 turret, well away from the rest of the crew, with only four Browning Mk II .303s for company. Once you're up at 26,000ft, the temperature is going to get rather frosty; you'll need to wear every item of clothing the RAF provides, but still expect your breath to be condensing and freezing around your oxygen mask, and don't be surprised if your tear ducts start to freeze. (You can wear goggles to prevent this, but they get in the way of good vision.) Preserve your night vision at all costs: stay away from bright lights prior to the operation, and don't stare at illuminated instrument panels for too long. In the air, use your peripheral vision to spot targets – the central part of your vision doesn't work well at night. Should you spot a night-fighter trying to sneak in, whip the turret around and lock onto him with your gyroscopic gun sight (GCS), which will help you apply the correct lead to hit a moving target. Then blaze away – hopefully a wall of .303 lead will send him off to target some other poor blighter.

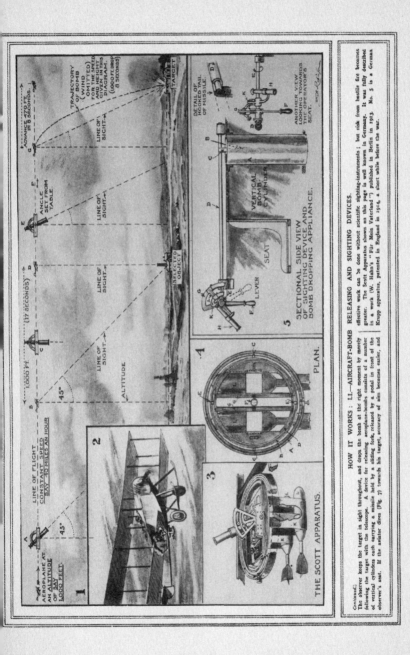

THE SCOTT APPARATUS.

SECTIONAL SIDE VIEW OF SIGHTING DEVICE AND BOMB DROPPING APPLIANCE.

PLAN.

HOW IT WORKS: LI.—AIRCRAFT-BOMB RELEASING AND SIGHTING DEVICES.

Continued.)
The observer keeps the target in sight throughout, and drops the bomb at the right moment by merely following the target with the telescope. A device for releasing aeroplane-bombs consists of a number of vertical cylinders each carrying a missile held by a sliding fork, released by a pedal in front of the observer's seat. If the aviator dives (Fig. 7) towards his target, accuracy of aim becomes easier, and

effective work can be done without scientific sighting-instruments; but risk from hostile fire becomes greater. The Scott Apparatus shown on this page is German. It was fully described in a work (W. Hahn's *Ueber das Problem des Fliegens* by Von Verland ?) published in Berlin in 1913. No. 5 is a German Krupp apparatus, patented in England in 1914, a short while before the war.

♦ Unstoppable airman: Douglas Bader (1910–82) ♦

RAF ace Group Captain Bader lost both legs in a plane crash in 1931. Not letting a niggling injury deter from his love of flying, Bader quickly got used to his prosthetic legs – referring to the crash as a 'bad show' – and retook his flight training to continue piloting for the RAF. Bader was invalided out against his will, but returned to the skies during the Second World War, his incredible aeronautical skills meaning that he whizzed through test flights and was cleared for active duty. Taking part in air actions over Dunkirk and in the Battle of Britain (1940), Bader notched up twenty solo kills before he was shot down over France, bailing out and losing one of his prosthetic legs in the process. The Germans had so much respect for Bader that they allowed the British to fly out a new leg for Bader, who promptly thanked them by trying to escape from the hospital. His repeated escape attempts led to him being sent to Colditz, remaining there until liberation. Leaving the RAF, Bader continued to fly for most of his life. He was knighted for his services to the disabled in 1976. All-round gentleman and scholar, Bader was just the person to have in your corner during a tight scrap.

Section Four
The Ocean Wave – Sea Warfare

• TAKE A DEPTH SOUNDING •

In a masted man-o'-war, you always need to know how much water is slopping beneath you. For this, you need a weighted 'sounding line' – a rope with a lead weight at one end, and marked at intervals with leather, serge or calico ties indicating depth in fathoms. (The knots indicate the depths 2, 3, 5, 7, 10, 13, 15, 17, and 20 fathoms.) As 'leadsman', stand to the side of the ship (steady now, or the blue will beckon) and lower the weight into the water, feeding the knots out through your hands until the rope slackens; announce 'by the mark' and read the depth off in fathoms. Shout 'by the deep' if you have to estimate the depth between two marks. Don't be tempted to just stand there, swinging the lead in the air and calling out fictitious depths – you might just coin a famous phrase.

• KEEL-HAUL AN OFFENDER •

On your Royal Navy warship in the early 1700s, firm discipline is all the swine understand, and a good keel-hauling will soon restore order. Take the offender and bind a rope around his waist (you can also tie his wrists together, for good measure). Now, drag him to the front of the ship and cast him into the water. Pay out the rope, and the blackguard will be dragged along the underneath of the vessel, ripping himself up on the barnacles and other rough stuff growing on the keel. Go too slowly, he'll drown, go too quickly, and he'll be torn to shreds. No more trouble from him if he survives, however.

• NAVIGATE USING A SEXTANT •

The stars and the sun never lie about their position, and neither will your trusty sextant, once you gain salty experience in its use. To find your latitude, set the index bar to zero degrees and put the sun shades into place – if you don't you'll burn your eyeballs out on a bright day. Now look at the sun through the telescope, then release the clamp on the index bar and start angling the bar until the sun, visually, is sitting on the horizon (courtesy of the sextant's mirrors). Now make a pendulum motion with the sextant, causing the sun to swing across the horizon, and when it is at its lowest point, tighten the index bar clamp and take a reading of the angle. The angle, plus the time the reading was taken, can be read against mariner's charts that tell you, within about 2 miles leeway, your degree of latitude.

♦ WANDERER AND WARRIOR: ♦
FRANCIS DRAKE (C. 1540–C. 1596)

Vice-Admiral of the British Navy, privateer and scourge of the Spanish, Francis Drake famously delayed confronting the Spanish Armada after it had been sighted approaching Plymouth in 1588. Using his superior knowledge of the tides to his advantage, Drake calmly concluded his game of bowls before turning his attentions to destroying the mighty fleet. Admired by men and women alike, the dashing seadog was knighted by Elizabeth I, the Virgin Queen, aboard his ship, the *Golden Hind*, in 1581, on his return from a circumnavigation of the globe (the first ever world sea voyage undertaken by a Brit). Throughout his days at sea, Drake amassed a fortune in the form of looted Spanish gold and treasure, his winning combination of luck and audacity always keeping him one league ahead. Drake was buried at sea in 1596. To this day, divers search for his remains and the legacy of adventure he left behind.

• CLIMB RIGGING EFFICIENTLY •

The 'rigging monkey' is a nimble chap to be sure. On a first-rate man-o'-war, he needs a head for heights – the mainmast can be 150ft tall – and have the stamina to traverse the tapestry of ropes, masts, yards, ratlines and shrouds that cross the sky above our heads. Furthermore, he has to do all this on a craft pitching upon Poseidon's seas, or shimmering with Jack Frost's ice. When he climbs, he goes hand over hand, never letting go with one hand until he has got a grip with the other. He also needs to plan his route carefully – many accidents happen when the fellow hasn't taken a logical route. Balance is essential, particular when stepping on the yards. The rigging monkey practices at low levels first, learning to balance naturally with the rocking of the ship, then works up to higher levels, where the undulations are felt to a great degree. Time served will turn the man from a hesitant, wobbling youth to a confident and nimble mariner.

(LC-USZC4-1887)

• DEAL WITH A MUTINY AT SEA •

The blackguards! I've taken them from the grim streets of some dirt-caked port town (often unwillingly, for sure) and given them the life of a mariner, but after years under my command, my sailors have risen in mutiny. No matter: I've dealt with such bounders before. First, ready yourself for a fight, if you want to avoid the fate of Captain Hugh Pigot, sliced and hacked to death by the crew of *Hermione* on 21 September 1797. Gather those loyal to you, promise them riches and favours, then get stuck in with cutlass and carbine. Take out the ringleaders – behead the serpent quickly – then slam the rest in the brig. Don't be too hot-headed now. Talk with the mutineers, and give some concessions to those of a more fair-minded nature. For the others, make an example. Hang 'em from the yards, or flog 'em with the cat o'nine tails (up to 300 lashes for the worst, although it will likely kill 'em). Or make 'em 'run the gauntlet' – walking slowly between two lines of men, each wielding a length of knotted rope. Humble or kill the wolves, and the rest of the crew will be lambs.

• AVOID SCURVY •

Scurvy: 'tis the plague of the oceans. First comes the black moods, and all your spirit and strength drains away through your boots. Then come the sores on the legs, bleeding from the teeth, pain in the bones, jaundice, fever and, if the sea gods be against you, a grim death and a quick drop into Davy Jones' locker. This dark malady usually visits us sailors after a few months at sea, when we've eaten nought but preserved meat. Two million of us possibly died of scurvy between 1500 and 1800, but thanks be to heav'n – the cure is simplicity itself: eat some lemons, oranges and other citrus fruits during the voyage. All them bones at the bottom of the sea but for a bit of fruit …

• BURY A BODY AT SEA •

Once a man's gone, he's gone. Keep him onboard and he'll begin to rot in days, so unless you are putting into port within twenty-four hours, he's going to have to go over the side (with due solemnity, of course). Stitch him into his hammock, and put the last stitch through his nose – if he's not quite passed over, he'll let you know at this point. Put two cannonballs in the bottom of the shroud; you don't want him to bob like a cork in the water. For the burial service, conducted on the main deck, the ship is usually cocked up to the weather, so it's motionless in the water. As signs of mourning, topgallant yards are a-cock-bill (set at an angle), lift lines out of trim, and the entry port on the starboard gangway is to windward, and open. Gather the crew on the deck, under command of the bosun. The deceased is placed on an eight-man mess table, the whole covered with a red ensign. Then the chaplain, captain, or other officer reads a passage of scripture and leads prayers. With the words 'We commit his body to the deep …' the mess table is upended over the side, and another mariner adds his bones to the sea.

• SURGERY AT SEA •

The ship's surgeon in Nelson's navy is typically a phlegmatic chap, used to decks awash with blood and buckets full of limbs. For many an injured sailor, this man represents the difference betwixt life and death, with the odds rather tilting towards the latter. Rat-infested ships, filled with the detritus of naval life, are ideal breeding grounds for post-surgery infection, but the surgeon will nevertheless engage in all manner of anatomical probing. Limb amputations are common following battle, using solid naval bow saws. Musket balls, grapeshot or wooden splinters embedded in flesh are removed (gently, for Christ's sake) using instruments such as bullet probes, bullet-extracting forceps and probe scissors. The pressure of skull compressions are relieved by trepanning – essentially drilling through the skull with a T-handled screw. Tasked with dentistry, the surgeon might spend his time profitably removing teeth with a tooth key or tooth forceps, or lancing oral boils with a gum lancet. Given sailors' preferred horizontal onshore activities, the surgeon will also be heavily engaged in genito-urinary treatments, such as inserting catheters to relieve bladder pressure. Variety, for the ship's surgeon, is indeed the spice of life, and frequently the spice of death for others.

(LC-USZ62-34397)

• MAKE A FIRE SHIP AND BREAK ENEMY LINES •

To make your medieval fire ship, first fill a vessel (of the required size) with oil, grease, rags, gunpowder and any other combustibles. If you are the fire starter, ensure that you have a ready escape route (such as between the two rearmost gun ports) and your escape boat is tethered an accessible distance away, ideally tied with chain and not flammable rope. If the winds are strong and just right, you can light the load then immediately abandon ship, allowing the winds to take the fire ship directly into the mass of enemy vessels. Otherwise, you have to stay aboard and steer, only abandoning ship just prior to impact with the enemy, or at least when your clothes begin to smoulder. Either way, your fire ship is best used against an enemy force at anchor, setting fire to your opponents or at least scattering them into confusion, where they can be picked off by the big guns of your non-blazing comrades.

• FIRE A FULL BROADSIDE •

A rippling broadside from a first-rate warship is enough to waken Poseidon himself from slumber. When more than twenty heavy cannon, including 32- and 24-pounders, thunder forth in one great shout, God forgive the souls on the receiving end. The French have their own version of the broadside. They like to fire on the ship's up roll; at the moment of ignition, therefore, the cannon are angled upwards, better able to demolish masts and rigging, and immobilise a ship. We prefer to take the battle to the men themselves. We generally like to fire on the down roll, blasting heavy ball and grape along and through the decks. If they don't die from the shot itself, the storm of splinters filling the air could at least take them out of the fight. Repeat as required, at least until the enemy warship is shattered beyond repair or flotation.

TRAFALGAR'S VICTOR:
LORD HORATIO NELSON (1758–1805)

Horatio Nelson took to the seas as a youth and soon gained a taste for the romance and adventure of the nautical life. When grounded after recovering from a serious fever, Nelson brought his British resolve to bear, vowing to overcome his weaknesses and return to the navy. Quickly proving himself patriotic and brave, Nelson was promoted to captain by 1779, still just 20 years old. Losing the sight in his right eye – soon followed by his right arm at the Battle of Santa Cruz de Tenerife (1797) – did not prevent Nelson from demonstrating his strategic military genius in the Battle of the Nile (1798), before returning to England a hero. It would be in 1805, however, that Nelson secured his historical reputation and safeguarded his beloved Britain against French invasion. Now commander-in-chief of the Royal Navy, Nelson set out on the *Victory* to finish Napoleon's navy at Cape Trafalgar. With battle raging, Nelson took a sniper bullet and suffered fatal injuries. Even then, he refused to give in until he had been assured of Britain's victory, his navy trouncing eighteen French ships without losing a single British vessel. A lover as well as a fighter, during his down time Nelson carried out an extended love affair with a married woman, Emma Hamilton, who bore him a daughter, Horatia.

◆ Useful nautical phrases ◆

Any good sailor knows that life at sea can be a dangerous
activity, especially if you aren't familiar with the lingo.
Try these seafaring phrases out next time you take to the
waters, many of which cut the mustard on dry land also:

First rate: ship armed with 100 or more guns
Keep your shirt on: avoiding ruining your shirt by
getting into a bust up
Know the ropes: literally knowing what each rope is
used for on board a ship
No room to swing a cat: not enough space to whip
someone with a cat o'nine tails
Sailing as the crow flies: straight on, following the
closest distance
Sun over the yard arm: method of telling the time for
first rum rations of the day

With these, everything'll be shipshape as long as you
'toe the line' and 'mind your ps and qs'.

• BOARD AN ENEMY SHIP •

Boarding an enemy warship in the Age of Sail is a perilous business. The enemy (doubtless the French, or those truculent Americans) now has gunpowder weapons, so if the battle isn't decided by cannon in the first place, the boarding party could be in for a rough ride from musket, carbine and pistol. The defenders might also string gunpowder grenades from the gunwales or yards, lighting the fuses so they detonate just as you clamber onto the ship's decks. Anyway, you signed up knowing the risks, so get stuck in. Your weapons are the following: cutlass or rapier, dagger (of assorted types), flintlock musket and pistol, blunderbuss shotgun (a real deck sweeper when needed), and a boarding axe (apply this liberally to doors, bulkheads, rigging and, when required, limbs and skulls). To board, your ship must either close right up to the side of the opponent (and hold close with grappling hooks), or you should take the boarding party in a small boat and attempt to climb aboard using grappling hooks. The former is best if you want to overwhelm the enemy with force. Once on deck, it's time to slash and hack your way to victory.

• DETECT A U-BOAT •

They're slippery, deadly beggars, gliding at more than 700ft depth (in the case of a Type VII U-boat) beneath the slate-grey waters of the Atlantic. Thankfully, its 1944 and you, as the commander of a convoy escort corvette, have a range of detection resources to hand. The first is airborne: aircraft-mounted centimetric radar can spot a surfaced U-boat at ranges of about 10–30 miles, depending on weather conditions and altitude. The aircrew can then either attack the sub directly, or transfer its position to you via radio. Other airborne detection systems include magnetic anomaly detection (MAD) equipment, and 'sonobuoys' – special sonar detection systems dropped into the water. You can also utilise the excellent 'Huff Duff' – or High-Frequency Direction Finder (HF/DF) – a shore- or ship-mounted system for triangulating a sub's position from its radio broadcasts. When you get close to the underwater foe, you can use ASDIC. This transmitter-receiver technology, mounted beneath the ship and known for its legendary 'ping', can detect and track a submerged U-boat by the equivalent of a sonar searchlight. When you finally have that 'blip' displayed on your screen, it's time to head in for the attack with depth charges, guns and every other sub-battering tool at your disposal.

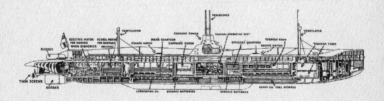

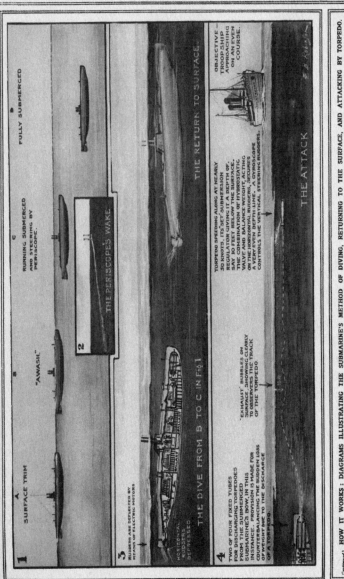

1 SURFACE TRIM

A

B "AWASH."

C RUNNING SUBMERGED AND STEERING BY PERISCOPE.

D FULLY SUBMERGED

RUDDERS ARE DEFLECTED BY MEANS OF ELECTRIC MOTORS

HORIZONTAL RUDDER DEPRESSED

THE DIVE FROM B TO C IN Fig 1

2 THE PERISCOPE'S WAKE

"EXHAUST" BUBBLES ON SURFACE SHOWING CLEARLY TO OBSERVERS THE TRACK OF THE TORPEDO.

THE RETURN TO SURFACE

OBJECTIVE — TROOP SHIP APPROACHING ON AN EVEN COURSE.

3 TWO OF FOUR FIXED TUBES FOR DISCHARGING TORPEDOES FROM THE SUBMERGED SUBMARINE. IN THIS INSTANCE, PROVISION IS MADE FOR COUNTERBALANCING THE SUDDEN LOSS OF WEIGHT DUE TO THE DISCHARGE OF A TORPEDO

4 TORPEDO SPEEDING ALONG AT NEARLY 30 KNOTS, ITS SET SUBMERSION REGULATOR GIVING IT A DEPTH OF, SAY, FIFTEEN FEET. EXAMPLE, THE COMBINATION OF HYDROSTATIC VALVE AND BALANCE WEIGHT, ACTING ON THE HORIZONTAL RUDDERS, SECURES A STEADY DEPTH LINE. A GYROSCOPE CONTROLS THE VERTICAL STEERING RUDDERS.

THE ATTACK

E. B. Robinson

[*continued.*] **HOW IT WORKS; DIAGRAMS ILLUSTRATING THE SUBMARINE'S METHOD OF DIVING, RETURNING TO THE SURFACE, AND ATTACKING BY TORPEDO.**

When a submarine commander observes an enemy vessel he submerges his boat whilst still at a distance from his target, and then approaches to a position within a firing-range of, say, 2000 yards (Fig. 5). If the sea be rough, and it is consequently difficult to observe small objects on its surface, he keeps the enemy under continual observation by means of his periscope, a vertical tube projecting above the surface of the water fitted with an arrangement of lenses whose design enables them to project the picture within the field of their object-glass on to a suitable lens under observation inside the vessel. If, however, it is inadvisable to show even a periscope, the object is approached in a series of "porpoise dives," observation being taken when the periscope is above the surface (Fig. 5).—[*Drawn by W. B. Robinson.*]

• SURVIVE A SHIPWRECK •

The tropics are a place of unparalleled beauty, unless you're shipwrecked there and have only your wits to survive on a hostile shoreline. Take some lessons from sailor Robert Drury, shipwrecked in the early 1700s on Madagascar, where he would spend fifteen years. The local king, Andriankirindra, took the British sailors captive, and when they tried to escape the ruler had most of them caught and executed (apart from Drury). Drury was then given to another king, Andriamivaro, as a slave. Realising that being valued was his best hope of survival, Drury put himself to work for his new master, eventually becoming the royal butcher. He held this position for ten years, until war broke out between Andriamivaro and other rulers on the island. Spurred by the conflict, and utilising information from a sympathetic emissary, Drury made good his escape and fled north, hiding either alone or mixing with various fugitive communities. He then managed to encounter an English captain and his ship, and Drury was able to return to England. What lessons of his adventure? First, be useful to your captives; second, make influential friends; third, look for the first opportunity for escape. Oh, but don't expect such experiences to be improving. Drury went on to become a slave trader and pirate.

Chapter II

British Food for British Men

Section One: Hunting

• Kill a mammoth •

Standing up to 11ft high, the mammoth is a tough kill for even the hardiest of us early human hunters. That's why, in most cases, we simply scavenge the carcasses of dead mammoths. If we fancy some fresher meat, however, the hunt's on. First, you need spears and lots of them, and you need to work in a pack. Use all available cover to get close to the shaggy brute, then throw or stab spears into his massive flank. Watch now – the injured animal and the rest of the herd are likely to panic, and it won't take much to snap your half-starved body with a massive tusk or thunderous foot. Another group of you should be positioned along the animal's flight path, to add more spears, weakening the creature until it falls and can be finished off. The truly modern hunter, however, uses branches of fire to scare a herd of mammoths over a steep cliff. The hunters better be hungry – weighing up to 6 tons, the mammoth's quite a meal.

• MAKE A FLINT SPEAR •

Sharpened and fire-hardened sticks are so Neanderthal. For the more up-to-date prehistoric hunters, however, the flint spear is a must. Making a fine spear head by 'pressure flaking' will guarantee you a good standing amongst the tribe, brutes that they are. Take a piece of flint that fits comfortably in the palm of your hand. Now you need a pressure flaking tool – another hard stone with a solid edge or a piece of antler will do. Hold the flint firmly in your hand or on a tree stump, and use the flaker to press hard on the edge of the flint. Little pieces can be pressed off, and in this way you can shape a flint spear head. Give it a broadleaf shape, with a shaped point and slashing sides to ensure penetration. Lash it to a long hardwood shaft, and you're ready for the kill.

◆ DINOSAUR HUNTER: WILLIAM BUCKLAND (1784–1856) ◆

Geologist and theologist William Buckland gave himself the difficult task of uniting evolutionary science and religion. He claimed that it was the Great Flood of the Bible that had brought about the current geology of Earth and caused sedimentation, a theory he felt was supported by his own work with fossils. Buckland was an avid collector of both fossils and animal specimens. It was through this interest that he developed an unsavoury taste for sampling as many species as he could get his hands on, aiming to eat every animal in existence. Rumours exist of by far the most bizarre morsel to pass Buckland's lips: the wizened heart of French King Louis XIV, which the Archbishop of York had in his collection of rare objects! Despite his peculiar tastes, Buckland was responsible for finding *Megalosaurus*, the first genus of dinosaur to be named. He became Dean of Westminster in 1845, a position he held until his death in 1856.

• MAKE A HUNTING BOW •

If you really want to do some damage, and at range, the bow is a must. (As it's the beginning of the second millennium CE, you'll have to wait 300 years before firearms come on the scene.) Bows all take skill and practice to make, but the self bow (made from a single piece of wood) is the easiest. You need a long (64–70in), straight piece of timber – yew, ash, maple, oak and elm are ideal – without defects and with a good continuous grain. Remove the bark carefully, then cut to length and width using a draw knife and a scraper, leaving a swelling in the middle for the palm of your hand. Cut angled nocks at the extremities of the bow and, with the bow under tension, string it with a sinew, rawhide or gut bowstring. If the bow is of the right dimensions, and you know how to use it, prey up to 200yds could be yours.

• KILL A WILD BOAR •

As a gentleman of lofty breeding, there's nothing more enjoyable than spending an afternoon skewering wild boar to death in the medieval English countryside. It's a man's game, make no mistake. A sturdy boar can weigh well over 200lb, run like lightning, fight like a demon and have razor-sharp tusks that can gore a man to death. (Even tropical tigers will avoid the fully grown adults.) The best way to hunt is from the back of a solid mount, armed with a boar spear – as well as a long shaft and a deep blade, it has a solid cross-guard to prevent the dying animal wriggling up the shaft in fury to get at you. First, use your 'limer' scent dogs to detect the boar, then unleash the pack of 'running hounds' to corner the savage boar and either bring it to bay or kill it in a ravenous fight. The manliest outcome, however, is for you to make the kill. Deliver a straight and vigorous trust down into the boar, ideally driving through its shoulder into the vital organs below. Keep it pinned down until the wriggling stops – never trust the boar until its eyes glaze over and its spirit runs off through the bush.

(LC-DIG-pga-05671)

• GO HUNTING WITH A PUNT GUN •

I'll never forget that crisp morning in 1815, my first foray out onto the water with a punt gun. Having been accustomed to shotguns, the punt gun rather unnerved my sense of self-preservation. After all, it was essentially an 11ft-long 2-gauge cannon packed with more than 1lb of shot and strapped to a tiny skiff boat. My quarry was a flock of geese on the River Derwent and, handled right, 'Old Thunderer' could cull fifty at a time. Steady nerves and hands were required – two small paddles to manoeuvre the boat into position, while I lay prone behind the gun (the position of the boat effectively aims the gun). Sandbags across the stock provided some recoil control, while my feet were braced against a kickboard. The moment came, and I pulled the trigger. The muzzle roared, the river exploded, and dozens of feathery bodies floated on the water. A good kill, despite the fact I'm now half deaf and my shoulder is bludgeoned blue.

• TAKE PART IN A VICTORIAN PHEASANT SHOOT •

A gentleman shows his breeding at the estate pheasant shoot as much as his skill with a gun. Be prepared for a full day and a big 'bag' – a three-day January shoot with the Prince of Wales (future King Edward VII and a formidable shot) might produce a kill of 4,000 pheasants, 650 rabbits and 250 hares. Work fluidly with your loaders – ideally two in number, taking the loaded gun with one hand while passing the empty weapon on with the other. Don't take your eye off the birds during this time; by locking your eyes on the prey, you'll make a better shot. Watch out for the low flyers – there are the beaters out there in the bush, and nothing quenches the fun like a dead commoner, so keep those muzzles up. Allow the keepers to dispatch the wounded birds briskly. Show a good stance when shooting the high overhead birds, dropping your weight onto the back leg, bending the front leg elegantly and keeping your head on the stock when rising up to the shot. When not shooting, immediately break the gun open, to show that it is safe. And at the end of the day, a brace of pheasant for beaters and loaders will show just what a magnanimous chap you are.

• FORM A 'PIG CLUB' •

When all you have is wartime rations to go on, start a Pig Club, is my advice. Here's how. You and your mates stump up the cash for a good old pig and knock up a basic sty from some solid bits of timber. They're hungry blighters, those pigs, but you can feed them with any old scraps from the kitchen, plus those from cafes, bakeries and any other establishment where you can go a-scrounging. (The government will also let you buy small sacks of corn, to boost the feeding.) Feed the porker up until he's nice and fat, then when he's ready take him to the slaughterhouse (the slaughterhouse tends to do ten pigs at a time). Half the pig goes to the government, and the remaining chops and bacon come back to you and club members. Add that rare fresh egg, and you've got the best bacon and eggs you'll ever taste.

• CHOOSE THE BEST DOG •

While women and money are a constant source of frustration, a good dog will be a redoubtable companion in both home and field. As a Victorian estate manager, in fact, several dogs will warrant service. The steely Jack Russell will be a fervent ratter, keeping down the vermin in the barns. For rough shooting around the woodland, a lively Spaniel will flush out the game nicely, while the English Pointer will indicate quarry with a rigid point (keep your gun up and ready). For gathering the birds shot on the wing, of course, there's none better than an energetic but stolid Labrador, that most faithful of retrievers. Your canine army will serve you through years, and, perhaps, provide you with that final companion as you stare into the dying embers of the fire.

• CHOOSE THE BEST BIG GAME GUN •

Heading on safari in Africa at the beginning of the twentieth century? If you are, then you'll need a true man's gun, one that nearly breaks your shoulder and could topple an oak tree. You could take the lead of an American, Theodore Roosevelt, who since 1904 has wielded a .405 Winchester, firing a 300-grain bullet at 2,230fps – that bullet will flip a charging lion backwards, so it's a dependable gun. Buying British, you can never go wrong with a large-calibre Rigby, Holland & Holland or Purdey – as attested to by their royal use. I can heartily recommend a .416 bolt-action, a 2-bore double-barrelled rifle or something capable of handling the .450 Nitro Express round, which will comfortably drop a bull elephant. Once you are suitably armed, look ahead to experiencing the beautiful wildlife of the African continent – and obliterating it.

◆ UNDER AFRICAN SKIES: FREDERICK SELOUS (1851–1917) ◆

An accomplished explorer, Frederick Selous, is long thought to be the basis of H. Rider Haggard's intrepid adventurer, Allan Quatermain. Born and educated in Britain, Selous harboured thoughts of becoming an explorer in Africa from a young age. When he was 19, Selous realised his dream and undertook his first voyage to South Africa. He spent much of the next twenty years killing wildlife across the world, especially drawn to the largely unknown territories of Africa, surveying the land and collecting ivory and plant and animal specimens for museums. He led many expeditions, always keeping good relations with the regions' leaders. After returning to Britain in 1892, he saw action in East Africa during the First World War (he was now in his 60s), when he was shot and killed by a German officer. An excellent example of British pluck and resilience – and known for his love of tea – Selous sums up the British colonial gentleman with style.

• Falconry – the noble pursuit •

As a medieval lord, falconry is just one pursuit that will separate you from the sod-cutting serfs you rule. To prepare you for the etiquette and intricacies of the pursuit, you could do no better than read *De Arte Venandi cum avibus* (On the Art of Hunting with Birds), written by Frederick II in the 1240s. This tome will introduce you to much of the art and the science of the hunting bird, and how to bend it to your will. You should invest prudently in your first bird. Note the list (introduced in the 1500s) of birds of prey permitted to social rank. A grovelling knave, for example, can only own a Kestrel, whereas an earl can possess a Peregrine Falcon, a king a Gyrfalcon and an emperor a Golden Eagle. Acquire a bird that is above your rank, and you could find yourself fined or imprisoned for your impudence. In the training of your falcon, be prepared for long boring hours 'waking the bird', sat alone with the bird on your gloved fist to get it used to your presence. Eventually, with guidance, you'll work up to bagging pigeon and rabbit, dazzling commoner and nobleman alike with your command of winged creatures.

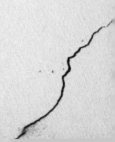

• Hunt a bear •

In the forests of medieval Scotland, you need your wits about you when hunting bear. Of course, you could opt for guile rather than strength – a sturdy lasso rope, strung and hidden across a bear track, can trap and hold a fully grown bear for you, ready for you and your party to finish it off later with a bear spear. (The spear has a broadleaf head for maximum damage, and a short cross-guard to help pin the creature in place, aided by jamming the butt of the spear against the ground.) For those hunters of more physical vigour, nothing beats the hunt with dogs. Sometimes a plucky terrier will suffice – it can distract the bear with its growling and barking, providing you with an opening to deliver an arrow or spear straight through the shoulder into the heart. On the other hand, you can hunt alongside a muscular pack of bear hounds, which will throw themselves en masse at the bear's head and lock on, immobilising it long enough for your spear strike. Should the hounds attack one by one, however, they are almost certain to die – once the bear has finished with the dogs, you might be next.

Section Two
Food and Drink

• PREHISTORIC BANQUET •

Just because you have an ill-developed frontal cortex and a lifespan of about twenty years, doesn't mean you can't eat with gusto. Basically stay close to your source of food – meat, fruit and vegetables will all rot quickly when taken from the wild, so you don't want to carry it on long journeys home. Typical meats are fish, deer, rabbit and the occasional mammoth, although the fact that you often burn more calories hunting the creatures than you get from them means you will stay forever skinny, and with appalling teeth. We also (your scientists now think) use a peppery spice like mustard to flavour the meat. Cooking, it has to be said, is a little crude. Animals are simply skinned (or de-feathered) and stuffed on the fire to roast, although wrapping them in clay can prevent their burning. Animals like tortoises and armadillos roast in their shells, hissing and smelling as they do. In terms of other foods, from the Neolithic onwards we've had more than you think: milk, crude forms of bread and alcohol, salt, and the usual collection of berries, seeds, wild vegetables and fruit. All good for a prehistoric banquet, although the terrible sanitation and hard living means you'll still be lucky to see your third decade.

◆ FIVE WEIRD THINGS EATEN IN OLDE ENGLAND ◆

Roasted peacock with its feathers stuck back on, to give the appearance of its being alive.
Live bird pie – a pie which, when cut into, released live birds from beneath the pastry.
Coqz Heaumez – a roast chicken, dressed up in helmet, shield and lance, astride the back of a roast pig.
Three-way fish – a fish cooked in three ways (tail boiled, middle roasted, head fried).
Singing chicken – a roast chicken filled with quicksilver and ground sulphur, and both openings tied tightly; when the mixture is heated, the escaping gas makes a singing sound, like the bird is alive. (Also highly toxic.)

• CANNIBAL COOKING •

Lest you be in doubt as to the savagery that lies beyond our shores, take heed of the words of Reverend David Cargill, a Methodist missionary to Rewa, Fiji, in 1839:

October 31st, 1839, Thursday. This morning we witnessed a shocking spectacle. Twenty (20) dead bodies of men, women and children were brought to Rewa as a present from Tanoa. They were distributed among the people to be cooked and eaten. They were dragged about in the water and on the beach. The children amused themselves by sporting with and mutilating the body of a little girl. A crowd of men and women maltreated the body of a grey-haired old man and that of a young woman. Human entrails were floating down the river in front of the mission premises. Mutilated limbs, heads, and trunks of the bodies of human beings have been floating about, and scenes of disgust and horror have been presented to our view in every direction. How true it is that the dark places of the earth are full of the habitations of cruelty.

• A MEAL FIT FOR A KING •

As a medieval king, your waistline and your power should grow commensurately. You've taken reign through blood and strife, so you should show equal commitment in clearing the king's table of its assorted and plentiful delicacies. As a decent benchmark, here look upon the dishes served for King Richard II in the late 1390s:

> Boiled wheat in venison, cured tongue, boiled meat, boar's head, fat capons, roasted swans, roasted herons, roasted pheasants, large, open tarts, and two subtleties [foods given the appearance of something else, or presented as if alive]. White meat in a sweet and sour sauce, white pudding, roasted piglets, roasted rabbits, roasted curlews, roasted marsh birds, roasted venison, roasted peacocks, roasted teals, large custard tart, fritters, and one subtlety. Dates in relish, violets, roasted cranes, roasted partridges, roasted peacocks, glazed with gold, roasted quails, roasted plovers, large game birds roasted, roasted rabbits, roasted larks, small meat pieces, apple or cheese fritters, fruit dumplings, quince dumplings, and two subtleties.

After-dinner mint, anyone?

• GO FORAGING ON CAMPAIGN •

On a long campaign, there's a natural limit to what foods your army can take with you. Foraging parties are consequently vital to keep men and animals fed and motivated. It won't be easy. If you're in enemy territory, the retreating army are likely to have destroyed crops and food stores along the way. Those civilians who remain will have hidden their foods well, so search every outbuilding, cupboard, floor space, tree and well. Take any food you can use, and destroy that which you can't – don't let pleas of mercy sway your war-hardened heart. Lallemand (1852), in *Principles of the Minor Operations of War*, explains the complexities of the foraging mission. Foraging should be preceded either by proper reconnaissance or by informed estimates of the likely yields of areas of ground. The foraging party needs to have sufficient men to gather crops and foodstuffs and the requisite horses and transportation to take it back with them, while an escort party provides all-round protection. Ideally, the foragers should never venture more than 10 miles from camp; any further is an unacceptable risk. There's no glamour in foraging, but once men begin to starve, the forager can become the greatest hero of all.

• MAKE THE MOST OF YOUR TRENCH RATIONS •

It's a beautiful evening over the Somme (apart from the occasional artillery fire, mud, ice and corpses), so why not regale your gastronomic senses with the finest trench fare. For starters, whet the appetite with a watery pea soup with floating horse-meat chunks (so that's where the old nag went), accented with nettles to increase the nutritional value. It's a somewhat familiar taste, given that the field kitchens use the same containers for everything (even the tea tastes of peas and horse). Now to the main course, so break out the fine china. Yes, it's Maconochie stew (again) – that tin of assorted beef, carrots and turnips, in varying degrees of flavour. One soldier commented, disrespectfully, that: 'Warmed in the tin, Machonochie was edible; cold it was a man-killer.' Pudding? Oh, hope that some family member has sent you some chocolate or cake in a package. If you've enjoyed the meal, you're in luck – you'll be having the same every day for the foreseeable future.

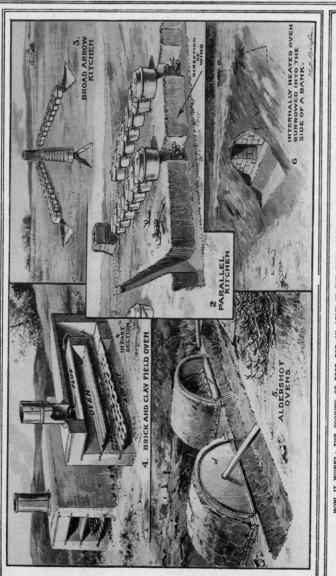

HOW IT WORKS : THE COOKING OF FOOD FOR AN ARMY IN THE FIELD—VARIOUS TYPES OF OVENS AND KITCHENS.

The fact that an Army fights on its stomach is nowhere better realised than in the British Army. As explained in the article opposite, Figs. 2, 3 and 4 above show types of ovens where the food is inside and the fire burns in an adjoining chamber; while Figs. 5 and 6 show another type where the fire is placed inside the oven and then withdrawn, whereupon the food is cooked in the oven thus heated.

The oven shown in Fig. 4 is for a more or less permanent camp ; while to build " Aldershot " ovens, as in Fig. 5, would also be the waste of time unless the troops were stationary for several days. The latest pattern oven—the " Aldershot " will bake 108 1½-lb. loaves in each batch. With a good heat rations for 220 men can be cooked in 2½ hours.

• Brew medieval ale •

The local water supply is often unpleasant (with side-effects of dysentery and cholera), so ale is the drink of choice in the medieval world. To brew, bring water (ideally soft water, which imparts a better taste) to the boil in a copper cauldron, add malt and simmer for several hours. Then move the liquid to a wooden barrel, and allow to cool to the warmth of a typical animal barn (about 60°F). Add a gruit (a flavouring, such as honey or cinnamon) and now leave to ferment for about six hours. Then cover with a cloth and leave for one to three days (brewing is a patient pursuit). Don't be tempted to give it a swish with a spoon – it won't brew things faster. After the waiting period, strain the ale three times through increasingly finer filters, then drink within a day or so … don't expect a crashing ride into drunkenness – most ales are so weak a child could handle them.

• USE THE RIGHT CUTLERY AT A GEORGIAN BANQUET •

Fresh back from the fighting in the Peninsula War, you now face a challenge of unparalleled social terror – using the right cutlery, crockery and glassware at a society banquet. Let's get our bearings. Everything is arranged around a service plate, on top of which sits a soup bowl. Now, look to the left. On the far left there should be a neatly folded napkin, and between that and the service plate are three forks (from left to right): fish fork, dinner fork, salad fork. Don't get cocky now, we're not even halfway through. Above the forks is a side plate with a butter knife, and above the service plate is a dessert spoon and cake knife. I know that your head is beginning to spin, but keep going man. To the right of the service plate are two knives: service knife and fish knife, with a soup spoon on the far right. Above the knives are arranged three glasses (left to right): water, white wine, red wine. You're good to go – just don't drop food, talk with your mouth full, place your elbows on the table, knock over a glass, be indiscreet in conversation or in any way enjoy yourself.

• THE EXPLORER'S MENU •

A life spent as an adventurer requires a strong stomach. For a start, you'll have to repress your fondness for domesticated animals. Horses, donkeys (whole roasted amongst the Persians, according to Herodotus), dogs and cats will all be on the menu in various parts of the world. Yet at least they are appetising. Out amongst the wild tribes, where literally nothing is wasted (although many things should be), you'll have to choke down all sorts of culinary horrors. In Central Asia, fermented mare's milk will produce the gag reflex even before it reaches your lips (think month-old yoghurt). In the tropics, diversity is the keyword. Expect to eat, depending on your company and the level of exigency, monkeys, snakes, rats, tarantulas and bats. The menu isn't always outlandish, however. In the Amazon in 1848–59, explorer and naturalist Walter Henry Bates (1825–92) was served a perfectly decent meal of chicken, fragrant rice, green peppers with lemon juice and succulent bananas. What's for pudding?

Chapter III

ADVENTURES
IN THE EMPIRE

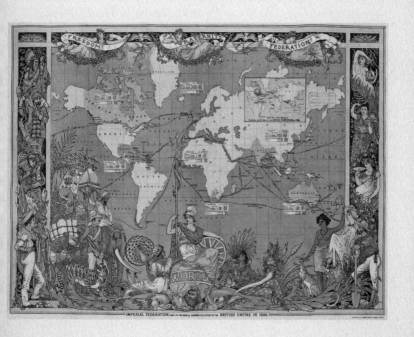

Section One
Dealing with the Locals

• PLAN A GRAND TOUR •

The seventeenth-century Grand Tour must be taken in the right
manner, and with the right attitude. Remember its purpose –
to broaden one's mind, tastes and cultural understanding via
a journey across the finest locations of continental Europe.
On the way you should take in the most sublime in art, scenery,
food and company, establishing yourself as a man of learning
and culture, all under the guidance of your tutor (also known as
the 'bear leader'). I would recommend the following itinerary,
pursued by many a young man of this time. Cross the Channel
to France, then journey to Paris for lessons in French art and
government. Next on to Geneva, Switzerland, then a coach
should take you on a voyage of discovery across the Alps into
northern Italy. Italy must be taken for all it has to offer – Venice,
Milan, Florence and, of course, Rome, will dazzle you with
their culture of antiquity. Back up north now to Germany
or Holland, then make your way home, to regale family and
friends with your adventures, and your now gushing knowledge
of all things European. Naturally, a secret trip to Dr Gilbert
will help with the unwelcome acquisition of a disease of Venus,
picked up in that Parisian gentlemen's club …

• SURVIVE GANG VIOLENCE IN BOSTON •

It's 1760 and you've just emigrated to Boston, USA. You'll soon discover that it's rough town, home to North End and South End gangs that regularly fight pitched battles over turf – mixing gallons of blood with the mud of the wheel-rutted streets. The night of 5 November is particularly perilous. If you're a Catholic, stay off the streets. The Protestant gangs will ride around in huge decorated wagons, bearing effigies of the Pope and Devil in cahoots. Some of the gang members will blow horns or conch shells, called Pope horns, and if they make a demand for money from you or your household, pay up willingly to keep your skull intact. Ironically, the Protestant gangs, united in their anti-Catholic sentiment, end the night in pitched battle with one another, leading to death and bloody injury. Arm yourself ready for defence – a stout club or cosh is the typical weapon of choice (leave the guns at home). If you are caught up in this, avoid being near the younger men (they're the ones more likely to conduct the fighting), but with the action numbering sometimes thousands of men, all up on Mill Creek, you'll need your wits and muscle to survive the day.

• UNSEEMLY NATIVE CUSTOMS TO AVOID •

The eighteenth-century explorer needs to prepare body and mind for the unusual customs of the benighted heathen abroad. Be prepared for shameful levels of nakedness. As Christopher Columbus said of the New World natives in 1494: 'They all go quite naked as their mothers bore them. None of them more than 30 years old, very well built, of very handsome bodies and very fine faces. They ought to be good servants and of good skill, for I see that they repeat very quickly whatever is said to them.' It gets worse, so breathe deep. Many natives in lands untouched by Christian grace have shocking piercings running through the private parts of their bodies. Some of the native males of North America and the Philippines, for instance, have tin nails driven through the penis. Naturally, as an emissary for King and Country, retain all appropriate levels of clothing at all times. Your attempts to ingratiate yourself with the native culture must have strict boundaries, and on no occasion expose your private parts, especially in the presence of a local jeweller.

• USEFUL PHRASES IN THE COLONIES •

As this is your first deployment to India, in the year of Our Lord 1880, you'll need to get up to speed with a whole new language – British colonial slang. Here's a few basics. Char (tea) – don't drink anything else! Loot – the plunder that is rightly yours, from the Hindu word *lut*. P&O – Peninsular and Oriental Steam Navigation Company (the likeliest way you travelled to India). Pukka sahib – excellent fellow (naturally, this is only used for European settlers). Punkah wallah – the dutiful fellow who operates the fan in your room. Following on from this: wallah – any person who performs an activity, e.g. a 'god wallah' or priest. Zenana – the apartment set aside for the fair-skinned women we have brought with us. Keep picking up the local language, but not too much if you want to avoid 'going native'.

• First Contact with the Natives •

It's a dangerous moment for all involved, so keep your powder dry. First contact with the natives of a strange and potentially hostile land needs to be managed with the carrot of commercial promise, and the stick of loaded musket. Upon first meeting, show your authority. Stand tall and give a nod of recognition to whatever stands before you. Keep your actions steady, your voice calm. The exchange of gifts can be invaluable for oiling the wheels of diplomacy. In the Americas, beads, feathers, metal, jewellery and cloth are all persuasive tokens; expect fruit, meats, fine handmade clothing, perhaps even a horse, in return. If you partake in ceremonies involving food, accept all that is given to you to eat – rejection is taken as an insult. Above all, appear unshockable, despite the many strange things you will see. The great Alfred Russell Wallace (1823–1913), while associating with the natives of South-East Asia, once remarked that 'I slept very comfortably with half a dozen smoke-dried human heads suspended over my head …'

• How to stand up to Native American torture •

It's 1750 and you've been caught by the Native Americans. They aren't happy – something about you shooting lots of their tribe – so expect two or three days of really decent torture. Unfortunately, your captors are fairly adept in the arts. They start by 'caressing' your body – lots of soft tissue blows that elicit substantial pain but cause no lasting damage. That doesn't last long. Pleasures that await you include: scalding with hot coals; ripped-out fingernails, strips of skin being peeled off, scalping, being forced to eat one's own flesh, and eventually fatal evisceration. The whole tribe will join in – the children, the little blighters, will twist your broken fingers, just for fun. They will give you food and drink, but only for you to stay alive longer. Here's the rub. They expect you to show courage and defiance during the whole process. As you are a British gentleman, that shouldn't be a problem.

• Hunt an Orang-Utan •

As Alfred Russell Wallace found, no voyage through the East Indies is complete without an afternoon spent slaying orang-utans. It is sportsmanlike to shoot them while feeding – blasting a large human-sized animal is made much easier when they are static, calm and unsuspecting, and also at ground level. Don't assume that the first shot will kill such a hefty beast – Mr Wallace required up to eight shots to finish off one stubborn individual. The wounded creatures will often take to the trees, and some will attempt to build nests high up in the branches in an attempt to recover from your noble efforts. If the creature has nestled itself in the canopy, send up a few more shots to try to dislodge it, or, better still, get a limber native to scale the tree and inspect. Note the dangers of the enterprise, however. Mr Wallace received a nasty twisted ankle slipping on some fallen trees, causing some distress to him and a brief reprieve for local wildlife.

• SURVIVAL SKILLS ON EXPLORATION •

Having travelled to many extreme lands, I have some hard-won advice to those venturing to regions far less temperate than sweet England. In the scorching desert, keep on layers of thin clothing – the Arabs do this to prevent sweat evaporation, thereby building a cooling layer against the skin. Use only seasoned goatskins to hold water, as those that are newly manufactured are rarely fully waterproof. Should you be cast into the white hell of the polar regions, the sufficiency of your supplies is critical. Take note of Ernest Shackleton's inventory for his journey to the Antarctic in 1914: thirty boxes of matches, $6\frac{1}{2}$ gallons of paraffin, one box of blue lights, two Primus stoves, 'a few spare socks', three cases of sledging rations (totalling 300 rations) – also acquire sturdy dogs to do the sledge pulling – 600 biscuits, one tin of Bovril cubes, and 36 gallons of water. Oh, and reindeer-skin sleeping bags are a comforting must when you are trying to prevent yourself freezing to death in some godforsaken cave or tent. The tropics bring different and assorted challenges. Biting insects are the constant curse. For this reason, build your sleeping quarters up in the trees on a platform above the ground, which is where the insects like to gather at night. Smear some petroleum grease on the supports, to prevent the greedy blighters climbing up to you. Whatever the region of your travels, take with you good humour and a durable attitude, and hopefully you'll see home once again.

Section Two
The Empire School for Business

• NEGOTIATE LIKE A GENTLEMAN IN INDIA •

When doing business in nineteenth-century India, it is sage to take on board the sterling observation of veteran colonial James Kerr of Glasgow, who noted that 'The natives of India, taken as a whole, are ignorant and superstitious, to a degree of which we can scarcely form any adequate conception. They are ignorant ... but *intelligent*.' When negotiating with a local, therefore, expect them to be vague with dates (for some reason they are not adept at handling our calendar), but they will be sharp concerning money. Haggle over price with acuity and perseverance. Kerr again: 'In all matters of business, in everything affecting their own interest, they display great practical acuteness. As bankers and shopkeepers they are not only clear-headed, but they have the spirit of patient perseverance in a high degree.' Be courteous but firm on your pricing, and for larger commercial transactions always have the confidence that the British will be the Indian's largest and most profitable trading partner (backed by a large army).

◆ FOUND A COLONY ◆

It is our God-given right to transform a superstitious and impoverished land into a beacon of law, order and commerce, all under the protective blanket of the British Empire. Thankfully, our experience in colonial outreach provides a wealth of guidance on how to establish any new colony:

Choose your battles. Don't try to colonise a developed, unified state (such is simply an invasion). Instead choose nations of either primitive native societies (such as North America) or those countries split between multiple self-interested rulers (India).

Move quickly. Don't think you are the only player in the field. In Africa, for example, the French (Algeria and Morocco), Belgians (Congo) and Germans (German East Africa) are all trying to take land for themselves, so send troops, civil servants and entrepreneurs in haste to any region or country still up for grabs.

Explore. Don't just go barging in with your army and navy. Send a few intrepid explorers to explore the region thoroughly, observe its customs and government, and define key commercial opportunities. If it looks promising, you're good to go.

Divide and rule. This is key. Send your emissaries to make commercial and territorial contracts with local rulers, appealing to their self-interest and promising to increase their power against rivals.

Establish a civil service and infrastructure. Give them roads, law, government administration, contracts and all the stuff and substance of the civilised world. Then no one will be able to accuse you of exploitation when, from time to time, your armed forces crush all those who have the temerity to complain about your unbidden residency in their country.

• REPRESENT A ROTTEN BOROUGH •

It's the eighteenth century, and you want a quick and easy way to take your place as a Member of Parliament. Taking charge of a rotten borough is a sterling route to achieving your goal. First, select an appropriate constituency, known for its tiny electorate but which still retains its representation by two MPs. Ideal constituencies include Old Sarum, Wiltshire (seven voters); Newton, Isle of Wight (twenty-three voters); Dunwich, Suffolk (thirty-two voters); and Plympton Erle, Devon (forty voters). As patron of a rotten borough, you can ensure the loyalty of your voters through a combination of 1: cash bribes (in many cases the locals will simply sell their votes to the highest bidder); 2: business bribes; 3: violence against any opposition. So, with a good handful of cash you can secure your place in one of the greatest democratic bodies in the world, providing you with countless opportunities to feather your nest. Take advantage of the times, however – the 1832 Reform Act will eliminate the rotten boroughs.

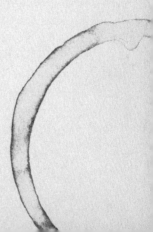

• MANAGE A TOBACCO PLANTATION •

Your tobacco plantation in the nineteenth-century Carolinas will become your fortune, but only if it is run appropriately. Of necessity, you need a workforce. Thankfully, one is acquired for free from African lands and supplied to your ports by enterprising traders. Purchase your slaves wisely. Unlike cotton plantations, when pure muscle matters more, tobacco harvesting and processing requires planters with discernment and intelligence, so choose slaves who have some aptitude. (Tobacco is a sensitive crop, requiring year-round monitoring.) Include women in the purchase, to provide breeding stock to perpetuate your workforce. Organise your workforce into 'gangs' of eight to ten slaves, under the supervision of either a white foreman or an experienced tenured slave. Each group should include a 'pace setter', a particularly hard-working slave who establishes productivity levels for the rest to follow. A typical cycle for your plantation will be: planting in January, harvesting in August/September, drying for a further 6–8 weeks, then off to market. The tobacco goes to market in 1,000lb+ 'hogsheads', and if you aren't paid in cash you'll be given a 'tobacco note' as a means to purchase goods from other merchants. Run it well, and you'll later return for visits to family in England with cash to burn, and some curious inflections to your previously English accent.

• THINK LIKE BRUNEL •

A giant of industry and empire, Isambard Kingdom Brunel (1806–59) has few challengers to greatness in his field. If you aspire to similar historical stature, here are some of Brunel's accomplishments that you'll have either to match or exceed (good luck with that, sir):

Bridges – If you are not impressed with Brunel's Clifton Suspension Bridge across the River Avon (and you will be), the Hanwell and Chippenham viaducts and bridges at Chepstow, Saltash and Maidenhead will surely change your mind.

Railways – As chief engineer to the Great Western Railway, Mr Brunel created a sinuous network of rail lines, tunnels, viaducts, bridges and stations across southern England and the Midlands. While he was at it, he introduced the broad-gauge line in favour of the previous standard gauge.

Tunnels – As an early project alongside his father, Brunel designed the Thames Tunnel from Rotherhithe to Wapping, completed in 1843. He also developed the Box Tunnel between Bath and Chippenham, nearly 2 miles in length.

Ships – Not content with re-engineering the land, Brunel also found new ways to conquer the seas. He designed the *Great Western*, the first transatlantic steamship (launched in 1837), and his *Great Britain* was the world's first iron-hulled, screw propeller-driven, steam-powered passenger liner.

◆ GAMBLING DEN: WILLIAM CROCKFORD (1775–1844) ◆

Beginning life as a humble fishmonger – the honest trade of his father – William Crockford won an immense sum of money (thought to have been earned from his skill at cards), which enabled him to set up an establishment more to his tastes: a gambling club. Crockford's members-only club soon became the most exclusive and sought-after club in London and was fraternised by the cream of British society, including several members of the aristocracy. Celebrities from all over Europe jockeyed to see and be seen at Crockfords, where they could carouse and gamble at ease, surrounded by splendour and discretion. Eager to take money out of the hands of those who saw little value in it, Crockford was able to retire with a fortune after running his club for thirteen years. However, habits of a lifetime are hard to break and Crockford subsequently lost most of the money he realised in the sale of his famous – and notorious – club.

(LC-DIG-ppmsca-28357)

◆ TOOL OF EMPIRE: THE EAST INDIA COMPANY ◆

Few companies in history have had the might and muscle of the Honourable East India Company (EIC). Established with royal charter in 1600, it built immense wealth through international trading in commodities such as tea, opium, cotton, silk and indigo dye. It also became an engine of British imperial expansion, not least by wielding its own private armies. The cash and cannon of the EIC were most influential in the Indian subcontinent, which the company entered in 1608. By the mid-nineteenth century, the company was the effective ruler of India, a position achieved as much through the ignition of gunpowder as through a sharp commercial acumen. The mighty did fall, however. In the 1870s and 1880s, various acts stripped the EIC of its privileged position and passed authority in India into the hands of the British government.

Chapter IV

AN ENGLISHMAN'S HOME IS HIS CASTLE

Section One
The Well-Planned Residence

• CAVE PAINTING: HOW TO / WHAT TO DRAW •

It's time to shake off your Neanderthal past, and enliven your cave dwelling with some choice works of art. If nothing else, they will confuse future generations – are they there to perk up a cave home, or do they serve some sort of religious purpose? Whatever you choose, theme is critical. Animals are a must – if you live in Europe, you can depict mammoths, horses, bison, aurochs, deer and birds. Throw in the odd human for good measure, but for some reason you can't quite depict these with the realism of the animals – make them more schematic (again, it will confuse the hell out of future anthropologists). To make the paintings, your palette includes red and yellow ochre, hematite, manganese oxide, chalk and charcoal, applied with hands, sticks or pieces of animal fur. Alternatively, you can etch the image directly into the stone, with antler or another piece of stone.

(LC-DIG-matpc-09947)

Think big – decorate walls and ceilings, and make the images nice and large (some of the bulls in Lascaux, France, are 17ft long, so don't be outdone). Once you've created your masterpiece, sit back by torchlight and enjoy the birth of the creative arts.

• SURVIVE A SIEGE •

If your castle or city is going to survive a medieval siege, you need forward planning and cooperation. Critical factors are, of course, water and food. When your castle was built, the Master Builder should have ensured an internal water supply, in the form of a well and rainfall collection gutters from the tops of towers. Don't rely on water supplies outside – these can be poisoned by the besiegers. (Store fire water ready to use for when the besiegers hurl fire bombs over your walls.) The inner bailey should feature plenty of space for growing vegetables, and a few livestock will add a bit of meat to your siege diet (you can also, eventually, eat the horses from the castle stables). Be tough on disease – if someone falls sick, hurl them from the castle if possible. At the very least, their carcass will inflict disease on the besiegers, thinning their numbers without so much as a fight. Also make sure that any minor entrances and exits, such as latrine outflows, are well and truly blocked and defended. Other than the survival basics, settle in for the long haul. Some sieges have gone on for more than a year, so let's hope you get on with everyone within the castle walls.

• Defend your castle •

Your castle is under attack from Welsh rebels, so you need to think clearly and tactically. Ideally, you want to prevent the attackers from crossing the outer curtain wall. Use your archers, firing through the arrow loops and from the crenellated battlements, to shower arrows down on the attackers as they struggle to cross the open killing ground. Drop rocks and other heavy objects from the walls; these will rebound off the battery (the angled piece at the bottom of the wall) and crash into the enemy, smashing legs and ankles. Be prepared to push away siege ladders as they are placed against the battlements, and if the crafty enemy wheel up siege towers, shower them with fire arrows – reduce them to ashes! Should, God forbid, the enemy manage to make his way to a gatehouse, drop boulders and hot oil down onto them through the 'murder holes' just in front of the portcullis. If the enemy is inside, you have to act with the speed of a scalded cat. Destroy the wooden walkways between the upper floors of the towers, obliging the enemy to cross the space using exposed outer steps or communal areas. Fight tooth and nail – after the bloody adventure of entering your castle, the enemy is unlikely to show you mercy should the castle fall.

• Implement a siege •

Castles are tough opponents, for sure; hence the siege might be your best option for cracking this nut. First, you have to isolate the castle from the outside world and protect yourself from attackers. Accomplish this with two lines (or rings) of defensive outworks, made from a combination of earthen banks and wooden palisades. The first line is the circumvallation, built between your army and the castle to keep the castle occupants in, and to protect you from their sudden assault. The second line – the contravallation – is placed between you and the outer world, to guard you from external support. Build your camp and ready your weapons between these two lines. Disease is your greatest enemy – dysentery and cholera can kill most of your soldiers over the duration of a long siege, especially once faeces and corpses pollute the local water supply. Return the conditions to the enemy by using your trebuchet to hurl rotting animal corpses over the castle walls. If you can find a water supply running into the castle, either cut it off or poison it. Try to get on good terms with the locals – you'll need to ensure a good long-term supply of food if you intend to starve the enemy into submission. You're in for the long haul, so put your feet up and enjoy the waiting game.

• STORM A CASTLE •

There are two main ways into a castle – through the walls or over the walls. Through the walls essentially means creating a breach. One method of this is undermining – you dig a tunnel under the walls, propping the roof up with wooden supports. Then you start a fire in the tunnel and retreat to a safe distance. The theory is that the fire burns away the wooden supports, the foundations of the castle wall are weakened at that point, and the walls collapse. Doesn't always work of course, what with the immense thickness of many castle walls. So, have you tried battering through the walls? You can either hurl missiles repeatedly at one section of the wall using the trebuchet, mangonel or ballista, or chip away with a battering ram, hoping that the edifice will eventually crumble. If it doesn't, then a bit of wall climbing is in order. 'Scalars', monkey-like individuals who climb assault ladders up and over the battlements, have to work fast and under showers of missiles, but if some can get over, they can consolidate a section of wall for others to follow. Roll up the siege towers to protect them, with the archers keeping the defenders' heads down. Lots of courage, an imperial ton of persistence and a dose of God's blessing, and you'll soon be inside, wading through the blood of the defeated.

• BUILD A SIEGE TOWER •

The siege tower, also known to us of the Middle Ages as the Belfry, is a monstrous engine of modern warfare. In essence it is a huge wheeled wooden tower, containing archers, pikemen and other warriors, as tall or taller than the castle wall it arrays itself against. Work the tower up to the wall, and those inside can engage the defenders with missiles, keeping the enemy busy while others fill in moats or attempt to ascend the walls with assault ladders. Some are even large enough to contain other engines of war, such as trebuchets. The tower is essentially a timber frame, wheeled on each corner. Platforms, connected by steps, are built at regular intervals up the tower, with openings for the occupants to engage from various heights. Note – the main defence against the siege tower is fire. For this reason, lag your tower in animal pelts filled with earth – these do not burn easily, so give you a measure of resistance. Be ambitious in scale and scope. The tower used at the Siege of Kenilworth in 1266 was big enough to house 200 archers and 11 catapults. Of course, one nasty pothole and the whole bugger can topple …

◆ Horse and Home ◆

Affection for one's pets is right and natural, although most would shy away from stuffing and mounting them in the home. Not so Lord Cardigan, aka Lieutenant-Colonel (later Lieutenant-General) James Brudenell, 7th Earl of Cardigan, although he had special reason to be fond of his horse, Ronald. This creature, a chestnut with white socks, 15.2 hands high, was born in 1850, and came to be Lord Cardigan's personal mount. It was on Ronald, that spirited soul, that Cardigan led the infamous Charge of the Light Brigade on 25 October 1854, at the Battle of Balaclava, Crimea. Incredibly, Ronald survived the charge, but of 673 horses that set off, 475 were killed and 42 were badly injured. The sterling beast eventually returned home to more peaceful times, passing away in 1872. This was actually four more years than his master – Cardigan died falling off another horse in 1868. Yet when Ronald passed away, thoughtful individuals had his head, a hoof and the tail mounted in Cardigan's family seat, Deene Park Manor in Northamptonshire. Hanging alongside other artefacts, such as Cardigan's uniforms and paintings by luminaries such as Joshua Reynolds and Thomas Gainsborough, Ronald is a touching, and rather unsettling, item of manly Victorian decoration.

• BUILD A CATHEDRAL •

You're a medieval master builder, tasked to build a cathedral to the glory of God (and to that of local nobles and ministers). Where on earth do you start? Labourers are required. First gather a select team of master craftsmen: quarryman, stone-cutter, roofer, sculptor, mason, blacksmith, glass-maker, carpenter and mortar maker. Each of these men will run a workshop of trusted men to handle their part of the building construction. The actual design of the cathedral will be decided by a body known as a chapter, who will work with an architect to create an inspirational masterpiece. Then to work. The foundation digging alone is an epic job, as the foundations might be up to 25ft deep, then legions of workers and apprentices will set to fulfilling the design. The blocks of stone are cut to order by the master quarrymen, using templates established by the master mason, and each block will be numbered and given a designated place in the cathedral. As the edifice rises up towards heaven, carpenters erect scaffolding for the workers. The work is tough, from sunrise to sunset, and takes many years. Norwich Cathedral, for example, was begun in 1096 but not completed until 1145. Masons, glaziers, jewellers and metalworkers transform the stone building into a shimmering place of worship, while plumbers cover the roof with lead. Once completed, step back and marvel at what you've created, if you've survived that long.

REACHING TO THE HEAVENS: CHRISTOPHER WREN (1632–1723)

(LC-DIG-ggbain-30741)

Knighted in 1673 for his massive contribution to British architecture, Sir Christopher Wren is perhaps best known for his exquisite opus in London, St Paul's Cathedral. The son of a clergyman, Wren grew up around the court of King Charles I until the Civil War broke out in 1642.

A promising mathematician and astronomer, whose cerebral brilliance meant he could have made a name for himself in any number of promising careers, Wren was thrust into the world of architecture in 1662, tasked with designing the Sheldonian Theatre in Oxford. It was in 1666 that Wren found an overwhelming need for his skills. The Great Fire of London had gutted much of the city, including St Paul's. Wren famously turned the cathedral's dilapidated spire into the graceful dome that remains one of London's best-loved sights. On his death in 1723, Wren became the first person to be buried in the cathedral, a permanent recognition of his architectural style that transformed the landscape of London.

• BUILD A FRONTIER LOG CABIN •

You've landed in New World Virginia, and you'll be food for
the wolves if you don't throw up a log cabin in double-quick
time for you and your family. If you're working alone, you've a
tough couple of days ahead of you. Ideally you should be using
flat, milled timber, but if this isn't available then you'll have to
cut, trim and notch a series of logs, which will lock together to
form the walls. A man on his own won't usually be able to build
such a cabin more than 6–8 logs high, and create a single inner
room about 12–16ft square. (Using other logs as skids, you will
be able to add additional logs on top.) Most cabins don't have
windows (it sure is gloomy inside), but if yours does, shutter
these with wood or animal skins, or even create crude windows
with translucent paper greased with animal fat (the fat for
waterproofing). Windproof the inner walls with clay, and apply
packed clay to form a hard floor. Use stone and clay to build a
hearth and chimney at one end of the cabin. To make the cabin
more cosy, try to build a sleeping loft as a second floor, reached
by wooden pegs hammered into the walls. You can then lie
there at night, listening to the wolves howl and wondering why
you ever got on that ship at Portsmouth.

• Create a well-stocked torture chamber •

As a torturer of the Inquisition, I can tell you that a medieval torture chamber is a work of some sophistication. Typically located well below ground, the eerie darkness is purposely lit with flickering candles to induce a sense of doom in the victim. The walls are not only immensely thick, but in the best chambers (such as in the papal palace at Avignon) they are specially curved, to reflect the screams of the tortured from wall to wall. In this way, no howls of torment reach the outer world. Make sure your torture chamber is stocked with all the best kit. One of the simplest devices is the *strappado*, a basic rope winch for dangling people by their arms, which are tied behind their backs (the dislocated shoulders bring forth many a confession). Other options are: the knee splitter (two spiked blocks of wood that are screwed onto the victim's knees, destroying them); the Judas chair (a spiked chair, onto which the victim is made to sit); the choke pear (a special device for splitting various orifices); a head screw (a screw for crushing the skull); and the redoubtable rack, for stretching the victim's joints to destruction. With such devices, an accurate and faithful confession will soon be forthcoming, and you can glow with pride in your Christian duty.

Section Two
Defending Hearth and Home

• SMOTHER AN INCENDIARY •

It's a blazing devil, and the Germans drop thousands of the blighters each raid. The B1-EL 1kg incendiary has a flammable body of Elektron (92 per cent Magnesium + 5 per cent aluminiun + 3 per cent zinc) with a thermite filling. Having smashed through your roof tiles and ignited on your hearth rug, it will burn at 5,400°F, setting fire to everything in its vicinity (that cheap lacquered card table is no great loss). Early official advice is no help. The information newsreels show a gentle lady dousing the incendiary with the jet of water from a stirrup pump, her husband thrusting the handle outside at a steady of 65 cycles per minute. Really, water's just going to make the bomb fizz, hiss and burn with greater frenzy. Far better is to use an incendiary scoop (basically a long shovel) to lift up the incendiary and drop it into a bucket

Use of the Redhill Container and Scoop.

of sand (tip sand over the bomb to snuff out the flames). Look lively – the quicker you can do this the better, before the Elektron really gets going. And don't forget the Germans are dropping other stuff too – an incendiary will be the least of your problems if a 2,000-pounder makes a visit.

• HOME FRONT FIRST AID •

You ain't always going to be able to help 'em. With the big stuff – 1,000-pounders or air-dropped landmines – all you might find are a few scraps of flesh and the odd limb. Yet as an ARP warden in 1940, you'll also see more injuries than old Dr Roberts saw in all the 1930s. Here you'll need to use the contents of your black metal first-aid box. You and most others won't have a clue about first aid to start with; that's why you need to read through the blue hardback *First Aid to the Injured* book in every tin. You won't be up to major surgery, but you'll be able to do enough to keep many people lively until the ambulance turns up. Torniquets will help stop someone bleeding to death, especially if bomb blast has whipped off a limb, and pressure on a wound with a shell dressing can stop

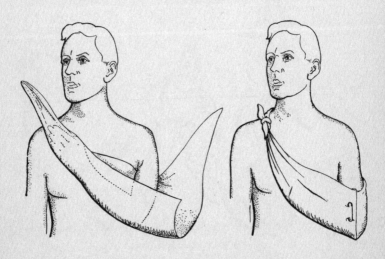

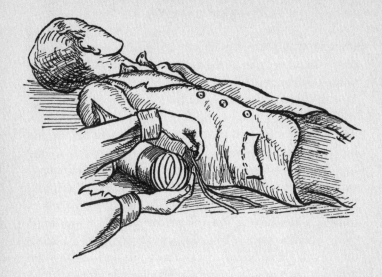

his or her claret draining off into the rubble. The triangular bandages will strap up a dislocated shoulder (common in people struck by falling rubble), whereas for little nicks and scratches a 'Germoplast' plaster will make the kids and the old folk feel better. The tin also has anti-gas ointment, to rub on gas burns. Thank the lord, the Huns haven't used this stuff yet, but they've dropped everything else …

• DEFUSE A UXB •

It's a job that will turn your hair white, but someone's got to do it. After every raid by the Germans, the city is littered with unexploded bombs (UXBs). Until they're defused and moved, life can't go on, including Mrs Braithwaite's milk deliveries. It's the boys of the bomb disposal squad who'll get the job done. These nimble-fingered types have a few options for turning the bomb into scrap metal. They can loosen and remove the fuse. Sounds simple enough, but the fiendish Boche introduced various anti-handling devices, which could detect and detonate the bomb when the thing was eventually moved. So, the boffins came up with solutions. You could fill the fuse pocket with liquid oxygen, freezing the fuse batteries for just long enough to remove the fuse. Or you could drill a hole in the bomb body and turn the explosive content to harmless mush by injecting super-heated steam. The final alternative is to give 1950s town planners more to do by simply clearing the area of people, stacking sandbags around the bomb, and setting the bugger off.

When a bomb falls in the open . . .

Hold a sandmat in front of your face . . .

Place it on the bomb . . .

and get away *quickly.*

How to enter a burning room.

The pump operator stays outside room.

Keep under cover as you attack bomb.

First check fire *caused* by fire bomb.

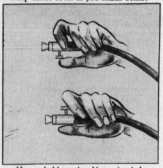

How to hold nozzle. Above, jet; below,
spray.

• BLACK OUT YOUR HOME •

Light is now the enemy. Open the parlour door at night, with that 60W bulb aglowing, and that could be all Fritz needs to send a 2,000lb redecorating device straight through your roof. So, according to the government regulations issued on 1 September 1939, you have to play your nightly part in the 'blackout'. Heavy-duty blackout curtains or blinds prevent light spilling from the windows, the edges sealed with brown paper and tape. Keep lights off as much as possible, and if you run a business, fit double doors to prevent light flooding out onto the street when someone enters or exits. If you're improperly blacked out, the ARP warden will let you know sharpish. Do it right, and you can rest assured that your utter boredom-by-candlelight will thwart those Heinkel navigators, thrumming through the air at 20,000ft above.

• Survive your bomb-damaged house •

With tons of masonry collapsed on top of you, you might think
this would be the time to panic. You'd be wrong. Panic will only
cause further indignities and problems, so get yourself and any
other hysterics under control. Hopefully you will be safely under
a Morrison shelter (essentially a steel cage in your living room,

COVER ONE CAN TAKE WHEN CAUGHT OUT OF DOORS

WALL

LARGE
TREE TRUNK

DITCH
BY ROAD

QUARRY

BANK
BY ROAD   CULVERT

Protect the Head when Sheltering in the Open.

useful up to that point for interning the kids) or in a shelter
under the stairs. Whatever you do, don't light up a Woodbine –
a leading cause of death following a house collapse is fire from
a gas leak. This being said, the gas leak itself kills lots of people,
as does drowning from burst water pipes. So if the air starts
to get thick with gas or water, try to move masonry enough to
create either an air hole or a drain off. If there are tiny cracks
to the outside world, push a stick or similar object through and
get waggling, to attract attention. Shining a torch through the
crack can do likewise, or hammer on a piece of metal or wood.
On a heavy raid night, it could be some time before rescue units
dig you out. Therefore respect the fact that you, your wife and
children might indeed have to talk. War is hell.

• BUILD/EQUIP AN ANDERSON SHELTER •

It might look like the type of shelter that couldn't stop a draught, but it may well save your life if properly built. The government supplies the basic materials – six curved corrugated steel panels, with steel plates at either end (one of them including a door). Bolted together, these form a shelter 6ft 6in by 4ft 6in, big enough to house six people in cosy proximity. But 'cosy' isn't the operative adjective here. The shelter needs to be buried a metre in the ground, and covered with a thick layer of dirt, meaning that life inside feels like you've become a cave-dwelling primitive. Some semblance of warmth is possible via a candle under a plant pot – sheer luxury. While away the hours in the damp and cold by playing charades, singing songs and cleaning each other of lice. Still, little but a direct hit will destroy the shelter, although after a heavy raid the same can't be said of your nerves.

The "Anderson" Steel Shelter Banked with Excavated Earth.

STOCKING THE REFUGE-ROOM

Particular attention should be paid to stocks of food, water both for drinking and extinguishing fires, first-aid outfit and tools for digging a way out.

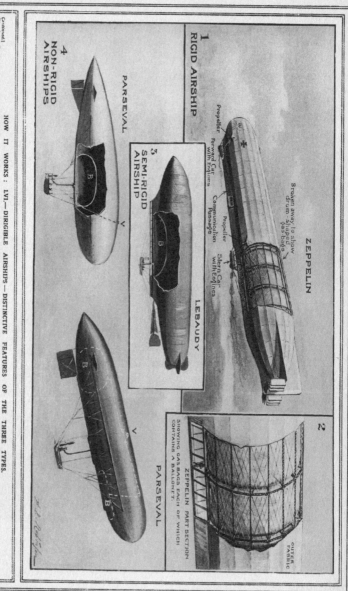

1
RIGID AIRSHIP

ZEPPELIN

Propeller
Forward Car
with Engines

Propeller

Broken away to show
drum-shaped
gas-bags

Stern Car
with Engines

Communication
Passage

5
SEMI-RIGID
AIRSHIP

LEBAUDY

4
NON-RIGID
AIRSHIPS

PARSEVAL

PARSEVAL

2
ZEPPELIN PART SECTION
SHOWING GAS BAGS EACH OF WHICH
CONTAINS A BALLONET.

OUTER
FABRIC

HOW IT WORKS: LVI.—DIRIGIBLE AIRSHIPS.—DISTINCTIVE FEATURES OF THE THREE TYPES.

[Continued.]
The Astra Torres gas-bag is of a peculiar section, as shown in Fig. 5. Permeable canvas partitions (A A) are stretched across the interior of the bag which form in section an inverted triangle. The apex of the triangle (which in this case is at the bottom) supports the cable carrying the cars containing the machinery, etc., and the sides of the triangle are therefore strengthened by planes of cable (Fig. 6). The Astra Torres has proved to be very fast and efficient, its qualifications in this direction being to some extent accounted for by the fact that the air-resistance on the cables is reduced to a minimum. Only the lines of rigid are exposed, as compared with the network of ropes which is to be found in all other types of non-rigid machines.

Chapter V

An Officer
and a Gentleman

Mens Sana in Corpore Sano

• The Charles Atlas fitness regime •

While not a Brit himself, Charles Atlas (1892–1972) is an excellent example of how a fellow should aim to make himself the best he can be. Having suffered the ignominy of having sand kicked in his face as a young man, Atlas (born Angelo Siciliano until he began to resemble the Greek Titan in build) turned himself into a walking advert for health, strength and fitness. Embarking on the Atlas regime means that you too become toned, tighter and stronger. By working on the strength of core muscles as well as surface muscles using his 'dynamic tension' techniques, you will gain strength and endurance, speed, power and contoured muscles. You will look and feel full of vim and vigour, ready to take on any challenge that awaits. What makes the Atlas fitness regime stand above similar fitness programs is the pride one can feel at turning oneself from a weakling to a hero, restoring one's honour and, as an aside, impressing the ladies.

• RUGGER AS A WAY TO MANLINESS •

We all know that the Battle of Waterloo was won 'on the playing fields of Eton'. That's because rugby is the consummate expression of manly virtues packaged into a single sport. First, it encourages boys to take physical punishment without self-pity or whimpering, exactly the sort of stiff upper lip they'll require when grapeshot has blown their legs off in the Crimea. Then there's team thinking – the boys must work together, tactically and spiritually, to defeat a common foe. Don't forget the desire to win. Never aspire to be gracious in defeat – it is far better for your captain to be carried aloft, throttling the desired cup, while your humbled opponents applaud politely yet inwardly despair. Rugger's also about the union of physical activity and divine virtue, as expressed by Charles Kingsley in 1879: 'games conduce, not merely to physical health, but to moral health'. Finally, and not without merit, there is nothing more compelling to the fairer sex than seeing a stout chap such as yourself wrestle another grown man to floor with grace and force, in the mud. No, nothing more manly than that.

"This is not the time to play Games" *(Lord Roberts)*

RUGBY·UNION·FOOTBALLERS
are
DOING·THEIR·DUTY
over 90% have enlisted

"Every player who represented England in Rugby international matches last year has joined the colours."—Extract from *The Times*, November 30, 1914.

BRITISH ATHLETES!
Will you follow this
GLORIOUS EXAMPLE?

• BEHAVE APPROPRIATELY IN THE OFFICER'S MESS •

The nineteenth-century officer's mess is a place where the elite of empire gather. Your reputation will be made or broken in the mess, so make yourself intimately familiar with the rules established by the mess committee, and adhere to them faithfully. As a priority, learn to hold your drink – even though fine spirits or wine might have reduced you to a mental age of 7, you still have to keep the clean lines of etiquette in conversation or deed. In conversation, avoid discussing religion, women, politics or, God forbid, the unseemly topic of money. Talking about your dogs, horses, cricket, polo, hunting, literature and military adventure is perfectly acceptable, however, as long as you deliver it with some sparkle. Regarding your mess financials, be diligent in settling your mess bill, paying for any crockery you break, and beware the mess bell (often made from an empty shell casing) – inadvertently ringing this bell results in your having to buy a round for the whole mess. When dining, don't light up your cigar until after dessert, and remember that the first toast of the evening is always the 'loyal toast' to the reigning monarch. Never has the need of relaxation been so rigorously enforced.

• TAKE THE WATERS •

A chap can easily find oneself having overindulged on the port and cheese. If so, taking the waters can buck one up marvellously. The waters are useful for any number of health problems and their healing properties can be either imbibed or bathed in for a full restorative cure. It is both the heat of these natural spas and the mineral content of the water that provides the satisfaction. Bathing in the warm, buoyant waters provides excellent relief for sore joints, especially during a brisk British winter, while the minerals give one the chance to top up on nutrients often lacking from the diet. Hold your nose and down the hatch. The spas of Leamington and Harrogate are fashionable enough, but for a truly healing experience, a gentleman heads to Bath. Here the joys of the Assembly Rooms combine with the spas to make one feel healed in body and mind.

• Queensberry Rules of Boxing •

John Douglas, the Marquess of Queensberry (whose son Bosie was infamously seduced by Oscar Wilde in 1895, which on Douglas' complaint ended up with Wilde serving time for gross indecency), devised the Marquess of Queensbury rules for boxing, a set of twelve rules that govern the sport:

1. Use a 24ft ring (approx.).
2. No clinching.
3. Three-minute rounds with one-minute breaks.
4. Ten seconds to return unassisted to standing position following a fall. If this happens, the round continues. If not, the fallen man can be counted out.
5. 'A man hanging on the ropes in a helpless state, with his toes off the ground, shall be considered down.'
6. No one can enter the ring during rounds.
7. If interference causes the match to be stopped, it will be rescheduled by the referee unless both men agree not to rematch.
8. New boxing gloves of good quality must be worn.
9. If a glove bursts or comes off, the referee must oversee its replacement to his satisfaction.
10. A man on one knee is considered down and if struck is entitled to the stakes.
11. No shoes or boots with spikes or sprigs are allowed.
12. The contest in all other respects to be governed by revised London Prize Ring Rules.

All in all, Queensbury's rules ensure a fair fight, meaning a British gent can pummel another man's head within the bounds of good conduct.

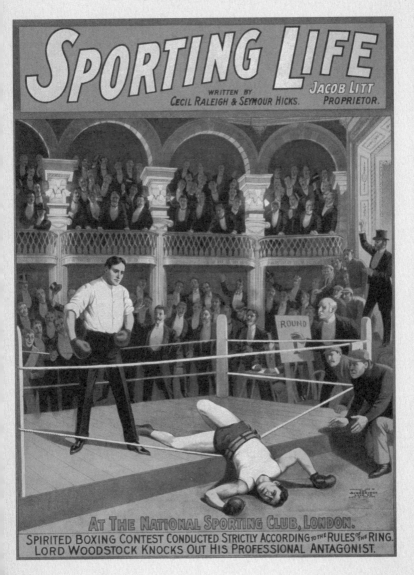

• WIN IN THE JOUST •

Sport of nobles, originating in the Middle Ages, the joust has been refined over time to become the pinnacle of any tournament. As you are a fourteenth-century knight, you must avoid the savagery of earlier jousts, with their remnants of heavy cavalry charges. The aim is to break your lance gracefully on your opponent's shield, unhorsing him if possible. You will no longer joust to kill and must remember to fight like a gentleman (it is now deemed less than chivalric to kill an opponent, hence the blunt edge to your lance). To ensure your win – and increase your chances to gain the favour of the lady for whom you ride – you need to get your strike in first. This weakens the aim and power of your opponent's blow. Aim for your opponent's torso, focusing on the heart (the waist-to-head target). Armour and his shield will prevent death; the result you want is to force the body backwards and sidewards, increasing the chances of his loosening his grip and falling. If you target the head, ensure your aim is good and your arm is strong. Remember, if you have issued a *pas d'armes*, you must take on any and all challengers who wish to compete.

• FIGHT IN THE MELEE •

No tournament would be complete without a melee, that most rustic and realistic of tournament battles. Stepping back from the romanticised chivalry of the joust, a melee gives the daring knight a chance to participate in no-holes-barred combat, often with any weapon one can lay his hands on. Knights generally fight in teams, either on foot or horseback, but it is every man for himself, as each knight you remove from the melee means glory and spoils for yourself. Bless their soft souls, women will not generally even watch a melee, its coarse brutality offending their delicate sensibilities. While risk is great, the rewards can be most profitable, as the capture of another knight means you can often earn a pretty penny by ransoming them back. However, the main draw is your chance to prove your worth in close combat over other knights and nobles. Surely there is no greater prize?

Section Two
A Matter of Honour

• DUEL WITH SWORDS •

For a true duel, one must be prepared beyond doubt for the outcome, be it life, injury or death. The goal is to restore your honour at any cost, which – any gent will agree – is well worth your life if it should come to that. Any bounder who refuses your pledge to gain satisfaction for the slight against your good name will have lost his good title forever. You will both need a second, a worthy chap whose duty it is to check the weapons, ensure a fair fight and even take your place should you be incapacitated. This being the case, choose a trusted friend who is ready on his feet and quick with a blade. (Your second will also work with his counterpart in an attempt to resolve the dispute before blows.) When you are agreed on the field of honour, you will meet there at dawn. This quiet time at an isolated place means you are less likely to be interrupted by pesky lawmen. It also gives

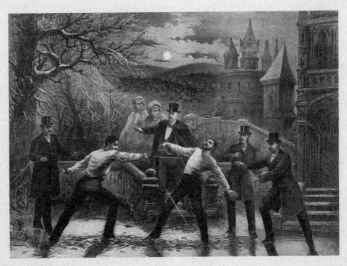

(Library of Congress)

one time to calm down after an impassioned argument or to sober up! Depending on the level of the slight, one might fight to first blood, to injury or to the death. If, during the duel, both men agree that it has been a fair fight and honour has been restored, it is perfectly acceptable to take a draught together. You have won each other's respect and, after all, duelling is thirsty work.

◆ STRANGER IN A STRANGE LAND: ◆ RICHARD THE LIONHEART (1157–99)

King of England from 1189–99, with tales of his courage echoing through the mists of time, Richard the Lionheart's actions during the Crusades in 1189–92 made the brave and determined king into the stuff of legend. The pious knight spent much of his reign abroad, risking life and limb to free Jerusalem and allow Christians access to the Holy Land. While King Richard did not win the Holy City, he successfully parlayed a truce with Saladin, the Muslim leader, to keep Jerusalem open to all pilgrims, winning the hearts of Christians and Muslims alike with his nobility and heroism. Also famous for his gallant manners, Richard could turn his hand to lyrical, romantic poetry and verse. Known as the supporter of Robin Hood against the tyrannical King John (Richard's brother), the Lionheart personifies medieval Britain at its most chivalric. Let's just overlook his continual war making, imprisonment and ransoming by the Austrians and Germans, and his inability to manage Britain's internal politics.

• DUEL WITH PISTOLS •

It now being the later part of the eighteenth century, one's weapon of choice for a duel has changed from the rapier or foil to the pistol. You will still demand satisfaction and choose a secluded field of honour, this time ensuring it is somewhere you are not likely to be overheard discharging your weapon. Your second will be even more important here. He will be responsible for ensuring your weapon – chosen from a matched brace of duelling pistols – is ready to fire. Agreeing the conditions of the duel is vital, as it wouldn't be cricket to impose each rule on the other chap. You and your challenger will start in a back-to-back position, holding your weapons cocked and ready to fire. When instructed, you will take a certain number of paces away from each other. There is always a risk of the other chap turning early to take a cheap shot, but you are a gentleman and must never let this possibility allow you to consider it yourself. When you reach the designated distance, turn and fire. Should one party be hit, the duel is over. Should you both miss, then you can either agree that the dispute has been resolved, or you can keep firing until one of you is struck. Please note: if you both miss more than three times then the whole matter becomes an embarrassment and etiquette requires that you stop and both retreat, alive but shamed.

(LC-DIG-ppmsca-26051)

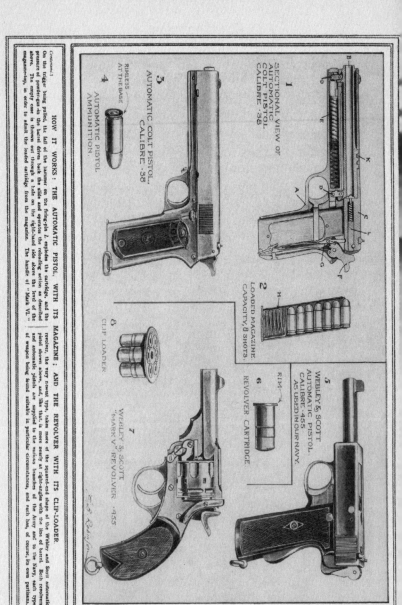

HOW IT WORKS: THE AUTOMATIC PISTOL, WITH ITS MAGAZINE; AND THE REVOLVER WITH ITS CLIP-LOADER.

[Continued.]

On the trigger being pulled, the fall of the hammer on the firing-pin Z explodes the cartridge, and the pressure of powder-gas—in the barrel drives back the slide and operates the reloading action as described above. The empty case is thrown out through a hole on the right-hand side above the level of the magazine-top, in order to admit the loaded cartridge from the magazine. The handle of "Mark VI."

revolver, the very newest type, takes most of the squared-end shape of the Webley and Scott automatic pistol shown above, and, like that, is more nearly at right-angles with the line of its barrel. Each revolver and automatic pistols are supplied for the various branches of the Army and to the Navy, each type of weapon being found suitable in particular circumstances, and each has, of course, its own partisans.

• CONVERSATIONAL RULES FOR THE GENTLEMAN •

Without the civilising presence of ladies, conversation between men can sometimes get passionate. Such fired speech is best avoided for gentlemen, as things said in the heat of the moment are hard to forgive or forget. By all means stick to your guns and uphold your opinion – you are no vacillating fop, after all – but aim to avoid confrontation on politics or religion. Instead, firmly turn the conversation to something lighter; the price of tobacco at Dunhill, perhaps. Make droll comments of course, but never laugh at your own jokes. You'll want to be conversant in a range of topics – science, industry, sport, literature and gaming are all popular. You don't have to know everything about each, but aim to know enough to get by on any subject. Be prepared to support any statements you make with opinions. Even if you are passionate about something, try not to hog the entire conversation. You don't want to be thought a bore. A word of warning: a chap can get a bit free after too many brandies. In this situation it is wise to keep delicate information to yourself. It's not as if you don't have any secrets, now is it?

• HOW AND WHEN TO SHAKE HANDS •

The handshake is a useful tool in any British gent's artillery. Keep it simple. Offer your right hand at waist height, grasping the proffered hand with a firm, yet comfortable grip. Shake in an upwards and downwards motion, but not too vehemently. Yield as soon as you feel the hand you are clasping start to pull away. If the shake goes on too long, it is perfectly acceptable to relax your grip, but try not to make this obvious. Depending on who you are shaking hands with, alter your handshake to suit. For formal business associates or introductions, keep it brief and not too familiar. If you are being reacquainted with an old friend, a two-hand shake might be fitting, but only if you know each other well. Let ladies lead the handshake, but avoid reducing your strength too much. You are a man, after all! Above all, remember the two most important rules. 1: maintain eye contact while shaking. 2: no one likes a sweaty palm.

(LC-USZC4-10976)

• Pipe smoking etiquette/rules •

There are few better ways of relaxing at the club than with a pipe in one hand, a paper in the other and a draught of scotch on the table in front of you. Of course, outside of the club, pipe smoking is best confined to your study. Be honest, old chap, the smell does rather linger, and it isn't fair to expect the wife to put up with it in every room. It is not done to smoke in company, especially if there are ladies present. However, if other members of the party light up first, especially the host, you may join them. If this is the case, remember to offer your companions some tobacco. It is also wise to wear a smoking jacket as this can be removed when in the company of others with acute olfactory senses. Always remember to remove your pipe from your mouth while speaking. If you are in the country, smoking in the street or on the golf course is permissible, but always seek permission from those you are with. In town, avoid smoking in the street. You are a gentleman, for goodness' sake, not a porter.

(LC-USZC4-10884)

• BEST INSULTS FROM HISTORY •

Us Brits are rarely stuck for something to say and can form a devastating insult if the situation requires one. Icons of the insult include the famously brusque Winston Churchill who, when told he was 'drunk, and what's more, you are disgustingly drunk', replied to the unfortunate lady 'you are ugly, and what's more, you are disgustingly ugly'. Bad enough, you might think? Not for Winston, who went on to say, 'But tomorrow I shall be sober and you will still be disgustingly ugly'. Smooth. Radical and politician John Wilkes gave this snappy retort to fellow politician John Montagu when told he would either die 'upon the gallows, or of syphilis': 'That will depend, my Lord, whether I embrace your principles, or your mistress.' The addition of 'my Lord' shows that however inflamed one's passions might be, a gentleman never forgets his manners.

A nod must also be given to Shakespeare, a true master of the putdown. Examples of such classics include 'whoreson', 'cream faced loon' and 'elvish-marked, abortive, rooting hog'!

• PURCHASE A COMMISSION •

Money cannot buy you love, health or happiness, but it can grease
the wheels of your rise through the officer class of the British
Army from 1661 to 1871. Essentially, every officer enters the army
at the lowest commissioned rank – ensign in the infantry, cornet
in the cavalry. Thereafter, a certain portion (about two-thirds)
of subsequent ranks are open to those with the means of
attaining them. (Note – you can't buy commissions in the Royal
Artillery, the Royal Engineers or the Royal Marines.) It's not a
cheap business, and the fees are dependent on the status of the
regiment and the rank to which you aspire. For example, a lowly
lieutenant's position in the infantry could be had for a humble
£700 (Victorian prices). Want to become a lieutenant-colonel in
the House Guards, however, and that will deplete your account
by £7,500. Thankfully, the costs are ameliorated by the fact that
you can sell the rank you are leaving. Some rail against the system,
but it means that we avoid (to some extent) all that meritocracy
nonsense, and can take the position we were born to hold.

(LC-USZC4-11975)

• ROUSE A COUNTRY TO WAR •

If you want a country to follow you into hell, pay heed to the
oratory of our own Winston Churchill, arguably the greatest
leader of the Second World War. At Britain's darkest hour,
surrounded by defeatism, Churchill always found the choice
phrase that stirred Britain's martial spirit. He was a master of
the fighting speech:

> We shall not flag or fail. We shall go on to the end. We shall fight in
> France, we shall fight on the seas and the oceans, we shall fight with
> growing confidence and growing strength in the air, we shall defend
> our island, whatever the cost may be. We shall fight on the beaches,
> we shall fight on the landing grounds, we shall fight in the fields and in
> the streets, we shall fight in the hills; we shall never surrender.

If this doesn't stir your blood, then Churchill's visions of the
future might do the job:

> Hitler knows that he will have to break us in this island or lose the war.
> If we can stand up to him, all Europe may be free and the life of the
> world may move forward into broad, sunlit uplands … Let us therefore
> brace ourselves to our duties, and so bear ourselves that, if the British
> Empire and its Commonwealth lasts for a thousand years, men will
> still say, 'This was their finest hour!'

If you haven't got a tear in your eye by now, then, sir, you have
no soul.

Section Three
Attracting the Fairer Sex

• WRITE A VICTORIAN LOVE LETTER •

Set aside fripperies here, as plain, yet heavy white or cream paper speaks volumes with its timeless simplicity. Leave the flowers and drawings to the ladies: all you need is a steady hand, black ink, red wax for sealing and perhaps a ribbon for that extra flourish.

Now, down to the tricky part; what to say! You will be wanting to express the deepest sensations of your heart, the sincerity of your affection and the constancy of your love. But don't forget to keep it restrained, especially if you aren't sure of her feelings. To avoid any embarrassing situations with the parents – who might well cast a glance over their daughter's letters – try this crafty technique much loved by amorous Victorians. Write your letter so that alternate lines express your feelings or denounce your feelings. The result should be something like this:

> *My feelings for you have not changed*
> until now as I see we can never be together
> *and never will while I remain a Christian.*
> When we last spoke I assured you of my intent;
> *now I see I must remind you that I love you utterly*
> no longer.

See, boys? Nothing to it. Just make sure your beau is clear on the code!

• MANAGE YOUR MOUSTACHE •

Now that you've managed to grow some decent facial hair, proving your manliness once and for all, it's time to make that unruly fluff do what you want. Start by purchasing a top-notch comb. Murdock of London do a spiffing number made of horn. Wax works wonders on stray hairs and keeps the old boy in place, even against those Channel winds. However, you need to be on the lookout when drinking your tea, as the heat and steam mean drips in your drink if care isn't taken! If, like all true Brits, you can't go without your chai, a moustache cup might be in order (invented by fellow Brit Harvey Adams in 1860). The moustache guard prevents your 'tache from making contact with the hot beverage, enabling you to relax and enjoy your brew. Thank God for British innovation!

◆ THE DISASTROUS MARRIAGES OF HENRY VIII ◆

When it comes to disastrous marriages, one need look no further than the British Royal Family. Perhaps the most notorious husband was Henry VIII, who tried six times to find the perfect wife. He failed each time, leaving behind the memorable verse commemorating the fate of his betrothed: 'Divorced, beheaded, died / Divorced, beheaded, survived.' Henry's crowning moment has to be his divorce from Catherine of Aragon, his first wife, who had previously been married to his brother, Arthur. A devout Catholic, Catherine refused point blank to the divorce, resulting in Henry – and the whole of England – leaving the Catholic Church and starting the Church of England and the Reformation. Was it worth it? Perhaps not. It took only three years from their marriage for wife number two, Anne Boleyn, to end up with her head on the block.

• SELECT AN APPROPRIATE WIFE •

One of the most important decisions a young Victorian buck can make – even more important than which club he joins – is the choice of a wife. Don't forget, divorce is frowned upon as well as ruddy expensive, so go for a modest woman who won't make a fuss if you are found having your needs met elsewhere. You'll want someone from a good family with the right connections. The next time you are attending a dance, take a moment to look for someone suitable. She will be properly chaperoned, of course, and suitably modest in mixed company. Secure an introduction and perhaps a dance to get her on her own. Attraction is ideal, but don't forget you'll need to be able to support her as well as any little terrors you'll be having. Your lovely lady's dowry has to be enough to get you started in married life. Of course, finances will be your department when you're hitched, so best to sort all that out with her father well in advance of the happy day.

• How to pay suitable compliments •

While a gentleman like yourself would never be so boorish as to offend a lady with rudeness, not paying an appropriate compliment can be almost as bad. Offering a compliment on how delightful someone looks is an easy choice, but by making it personal, it can work wonders. Every lady will have heard those obvious clichés on her becoming dress and divine bonnet, so aim for something more sophisticated. Look more closely and compliment something about her that you really like. Paired with a kiss to the back of the hand while gazing into her eyes, your compliment won't be forgotten in a hurry! And don't forget that compliments aren't just for the ladies. Every chap needs to feel admired now and again, so if you mean it, say it. You can't go wrong with classics like 'You, Sir, are a gentleman and a scholar'. You'll quite make that person's day. By the way, if you are on the receiving end of a compliment, the acceptable response is simply 'thank you' – don't be too gushing.

"PROMISE ME THAT YOUR HUSBAND SHALL KNOW NOTHING OF WHAT I HAVE TOLD YOU TO-NIGHT."

(LC-USZ6-430)

• WRITE A LOVE POEM •

Aah, the love poem. The gallant outpourings of a man's heart to the love of his life, all written in perfect iambic pentameter and rhyme. A tricky business, but one that can be negotiated by finding a mentor. Chances are your beau prefers the literary musings of one poet in particular. This is the style to go for. Popular choices include Byron, Keats and Shelley and never forget the patron of the love sonnet, Will Shakespeare. Don't be tempted to cheat and plagiarise some other fellow's work. Even if your intended doesn't recognise it, her friends might and you can't expect your sweetheart not to show it off, now, can you? If all else fails, just be honest; she will recognise your true feelings shining through. Chose a clear sentiment, select sparkling and erudite adjectives, and throw in a few classical allusions to demonstrate your learning. And don't forget, you can't go wrong with a good simile. If her smile is as sweet as sugar plums, be a man and tell her.

◆ SOCIETY TEMPTRESS: KITTY FISHER (D. 1767) ◆

An infamous eighteenth-century courtesan, Kitty Fisher intrigued and scandalised British society. When asked by Lady Coventry – with whom Kitty held a long-standing public row – where her dress was from, Kitty replied that Lady Coventry best ask her husband, as it was he who had bought it for her! Far more than just a pretty, popular pastime, Kitty used her coquetry to her own advantage by becoming the favourite model of several influential eighteenth-century painters. One witty portrait owned by the National Portrait Gallery in London depicts Kitty smiling coyly at her painter as she demurely holds a lace scarf to her bosom. Next to her, a kitten plunders a fishbowl for a treat; look closely at the bowl, and you'll see lusty spectators gazing in through the window. Kitty was famously dismissed by Casanova in 1763, but this slight did her no harm and she ended her career in the oldest profession by marrying a Member of Parliament in 1766.

(LC-USZ62-132018)

• WIN OVER THE FAMILY •

Meeting the family can be a delicate matter, especially if one's past reputation is … a touch blemished. Never fear. By taking control of the situation, you can mend any amount of damage. Address areas of concern before they are even brought up, then stress what a changed man you are since you met their beloved daughter. Even if there aren't any nasty little secrets lurking in your past (well done), you will still want to make the best impression you can, so now is not the time to act shy. Ask your lady friend about her family's interests and bone up on a few conversational topics, remembering to stay away from anything controversial. Sport can work well if the old man isn't warming up, and her mother will be putty in your hands after a few compliments on her stylish home. Consider casual ways to let slip information on your education, position in society and any charitable deeds in which you engage your time. And never forget the salient point: don't leave them in any doubt that your intentions towards their daughter are anything but honourable!

• THE GENTLEMAN'S STAG NIGHT •

The stag night, for the Victorian gentleman, is an evening of solid manliness. It frequently takes the form of a black-tie dinner, hosted by your father and open to a select few friends. While you might have been hoping for some ribald fun on the streets and in the clubs of London, the evening is more likely to consist of gentle drunkenness, cigars and some suggestive jokes (to which knowing and stentorian laughter is the correct response). The party is also an opportunity for you to invite over those gentlemen of whom your fiancée might not entirely approve. The evening is a clear sign to them that your days of high-living are over, and that you are about to become a serious society gentleman. After some fine food and good wine, you can reflect on your imminent future through a light fog of cigar smoke and mild alcoholic depression. Still, don't worry about your wife having a similar engagement – it won't be until the 1960s that the hen party is created.

◆ THE TORTURED POET: LORD BYRON (1788–1824) ◆

Lord Byron is legendary for being one of the most profligate, flamboyant and debauched men of his age. His notoriety combines winningly with his superbly eloquent Romantic poetry, which is brooding, yet beautiful, often with a perceptive underlying social commentary. His genius came in part from seeking the very life he aspired to, yet never achieved: that of perfect, unattainable love. Instead Byron discovered in himself and others the darker side of human nature. Rumours of affairs, incest and even sodomy led to our hero being cast out of Britain by the very society that had previously fuelled his passions. Byron left Britain in 1816, never to return. His poems grew in mastery and popularity, making the Byronic hero of literature – personified in his own angelic looks, tortured soul and dissipated personality – a muse for great literature ever since. Dying in Greece in 1824, where his lungs remained when his body was returned to British shores, the scandal that blackened his name was not washed away by his death, and Byron was refused burial in Westminster Abbey. A memorial there now marks the life of this inspirational, infamous romantic, beloved as one of the greatest British poets.

(LC-USZ62-99928)

Section Four
Wardrobe Hints for British Men

• THE VIGOROUS CODPIECE •

An essential item in the wardrobe of every sixteenth-century gent, the codpiece (from the Middle English 'cod', meaning 'scrotum') acts as a modest covering of an otherwise exposed area and an effective way to enhance or emphasise your manhood. It originated in the fourteenth century, when a gentleman's hose consisted of two separate legs, the groin area covered with a thin linen undergarment. The shortening of men's jackets in the Renaissance therefore resulted in an exposed groin, and some unpleasant exposures when men mounted their horses.

To preserve their dignity, the codpiece was born, at first a concealing piece of fabric but later an accoutrement to draw the eye and cause a gasp. As it's the sixteenth century, you can choose from a provocative range of uprising designs made of metal, leather or thick cloth – one surprising variant even has a man's face on its tip. When the ladies reach for their smelling salts and effect a swoon, you'll know that you've dressed to impress.

HENRY VIII

• Dress like a dandy •

You're following in the rich tradition of the dandy, established in the 1790s in France and England. Remember that despite your rather humble origins in the middle class, the true dandy seeks to imitate the dress and inflections of the aristocracy, celebrating the aesthetic of the gentleman while also affecting a cynical disdain for the ways of the modern world. Remember the words of Charles Baudelaire:

> These beings have no other status, but that of cultivating the idea of beauty in their own persons, of satisfying their passions, of feeling and thinking … Contrary to what many thoughtless people seem to believe, dandyism is not even an excessive delight in clothes and material elegance. For the perfect dandy, these things are no more than the symbol of the aristocratic superiority of his mind.

As the modern British dandy, you can model yourself on the likes of George Bryan 'Beau' Brummell (1778–1840). Ensure that you are immaculately dressed, with all shirts spotless and starched, a diligently brushed jacket, mirror-polished

boots and an exquisitely tied cravat. Lace accents around the collar, breast and neck of a shirt gives you a poetical, rakish look loved by the ladies. Gloves and accessories must be achingly fashionable. As Thomas Carlyle remarked in 1836: 'A Dandy is a clothes-wearing Man, a Man whose trade, office and existence consists in the wearing of Clothes.'

◆ IMMACULATE CONCEPTION: ◆
BEAU BRUMMELL (1778–1840)

Fashion icon of Regency England, Beau Brummell cut a dash through fashionable society in the early nineteenth century, becoming a close friend and confidante of the Prince Regent (later George IV). The original dandy, Brummell revolutionised men's clothing, moving it away from the previously fashionable – yet vulgar – style to his preferred understated and immaculate tailoring. A man who understood the importance of a well-tied cravat, Brummell was reported to have spent up to five hours a day at his toilette, before indulging in the usual pursuits of gambling, drinking and womanising. Later gaining a commission with the 10th Royal Hussars, it would be his self-absorption and uncompromising attention to style that led to his increasing debts and bad name. His famously caustic tongue also earned him enemies and Brummell even turned on the Prince Regent, causing society to shift against him. Finally fleeing to France to avoid an ignominious end in a debtor's prison, Brummell died alone and penniless in a French asylum in 1840, a poignant reminder of how unpaid debts of honour always catch up with you at the end.

• DRESS LIKE A VIKING KING •

As *konungr* (a Viking leader), you needn't be afraid to experiment with colour. Silver and gold thread sets off luxurious rich tones of red and purple perfectly. Top off your wool trousers with a tunic, followed by a wool or leather cloak to protect you from the biting winds of the fjords, fastened with a brooch or metal clasp. Add a silver armband or two to show your wealth. Keep your feet warm and dry with leather or goatskin shoes. Unlike your men, you can afford to be properly kitted out for battle. This means leather body protection or *brynie* (mail armour) if you can afford it. The signature Viking helmet would be worn by the king, of course, and you'll need a shield to protect you from arrows and axes. If you take a death-blow, hold on to your sword as you'll need it, and all the jewellery you've amassed from pillaging, to keep you company on your burial ship. Despite popular opinion, a Viking king's appearance should be well-groomed. Use a bone comb for your hair and beard and keep them clean. Even Cnut/Canute the Great took time out from ruling the North Sea Empire for his weekly 'washing day'!

• ITEMS WORN BY A MEDIEVAL KING •

Surcoat – made of cloth and in a vivid regal colour, such as scarlet or blue.

Shoes – quality leather, with the toe extending to a refined point.

Breeches and stockings – of the same colour, and with the breeches overlapping and holding up the socks.

Lots of fur – a fur mantle thrown around the shoulders, made from some now-endangered animal such as mink or sable, and surcoat might be trimmed in ermine.

Headdress – lots of variety here, but made from high-quality felt, otter, wool, cotton or goatskin.

Bling – abound with jewellery – lots of gold, silver and precious clothes dotted around your clothing, and a massive gold belt for good measure.

Oh, and nothing says 'I'm a king' like a crown. A crown described from the 1399 inventory of Richard II portrays a typical (i.e nothing special) crown thus:

> Item, a crown of eleven plaques [segment of the crown's circlet], set with eleven sapphires, thirty-three balas rubies, a hundred and thirty-two pearls, thirty-three diamonds, eight of them imitation gems. Item, six fleurons [lily-shaped pinnacles extending up from the circlet] each with a balas ruby, five sapphires, and nine pearls, seven pearls in all being missing. Item, six smaller fleurons, each with a sapphire, four small balas rubies, an emerald (one emerald being missing) and two little pearls in each, weighing 5 marks 7 oz.

• DRESS LIKE A REDCOAT •

The pride one feels when striding about in the trademark red coat is matched only by the terror the blaze of colour is capable of striking into the cold heart of the enemy. Traditionally the colour of higher ranks, scarlet was adopted by most regiments from the eighteenth century. As an infantryman, your blazer needs to be kept in good condition. The contrasting facings for an English and Welshman are white, giving your new jacket a smart and pleasing swagger. Do not fear that the bright colour will make you an easy target on the battlefield. You'll be covered in black powder from musket fire soon enough and the cheap red vegetable dyes fade quickly. A chap might imagine that bloodstains will fade in; they can leave unpleasant blackish stains that you'll be picked up for on parade. All in all, however, the redcoat works best as an enduring symbol of the empire.

(LC-DIG-ppmsca-27854)

• DRESS FOR DINNER •

You may have a man to help you dress, in which case over to him. If not, ensure that you keep a good tailor, as a well-cut dinner jacket speaks volumes and is worth any expense. Dinnerwear etiquette is formal. Black cloth trousers, a black tailcoat and a black waistcoat (possibly white, if one doesn't mind emulating the Americans) are essential and will ever remain so. For dinner, a white necktie is preferred. Keep shirts plain and functional, but above all, spotlessly clean. Gloves – also pure white – must be worn until sitting down to dinner. For tea parties, one can get away without the formality of gloves, but if you are ever unsure, it is best to wear them. Avoid all eccentricities at the dinner table unless you purposely want to convey a foppish air. Keep jewellery discreet – a fine pair of cufflinks and a venerable pocket watch will strike the right air.

• Shine your shoes like a soldier •

Never underestimate the importance of properly shined shoes. By following these tips, you'll be the proud owner of the shiniest shoes outside the British Armed Forces. It's not just a question of spit and polish, you know. You'll need lots of newspaper or an old blanket for protection (although the best place for shoe shining is outside). Find a nice soft rag. Wax polish that matches your shoes, a brush and shoe cleaner to get rid of the mud are also required. Start by cleaning off all the mud, blood or whatever else is mucking up your footwear, then get to work. Wrap the rag around your forefinger so that there are no wrinkles. Then choose whether to go for water or spit to wet the rag, before dipping into the polish and applying to the shoes. Using water allows most of the polish to end up on the shoes as intended, instead of soaking into the rag. When you have applied polish all over the shoe, taking care to cover any cracks, give it ten minutes or so for the polish to sink in but not long enough to dry completely. This is where the elbow grease comes in. You now have to buff your shoes with the brush until they shine like a new Rolls-Royce. This may take several applications depending on the state of your shoes. Hard work, but true spit and polish.

• WET SHAVE •

If your barber is too busy to fit you in, here's how to wet shave yourself to perfection. Hot towels serve an important purpose. They soften your skin and hair, making the shave smoother. An alternative is to thoroughly soak your skin with warm water, then give your face a clean with some Ponds or Imperial Leather. Next up, apply the cream lavishly to the beard. Geo. F. Trumper or Taylor of Old Bond Street stock the finest soaps and badger's hair makes the finest brushes. For a razor, select a lethally sharp straight-edge cut-throat variety. Fine examples, with bone, horn or ivory handles, can be bought from the likes of IXL George Wostenholm & Son and Thomas Turner & Co., and honed to perfection with repeated strokes along a strop. Of course, a steady hand is needed, so if you were a bit liberal with the grape or grain the night before, wet shaving is best avoided! Remember to go with the direction of the hair and keep both skin and razor moist and well-coated throughout. Finish with alternating hot and cold rinses to close pores and remove all traces of soap. Treat your skin – and the ladies – to a splash of cologne. You're now ready to face the world.

• CHOOSE AN APPROPRIATE WIG •

Your wig will bring you visual distinction, and that curious mixture of flamboyance and authority that you need to cut a dash in society. As it is the 1660s, and the Restoration of Charles II has brought some life back into the court and society, shoulder-length periwigs are currently the rage. The very best examples, made by a recognised wigmakers' guild, are those of real human hair (for the lesser orders, goat and horse hair will have to suffice). Ensure that your wig is properly powdered to ensure its fragrance and clean appearance. (Wig powder might be violet, blue, pink or yellow, but it is generally best to keep to white or ivory.) As well as helping you to cut a dash, your wig serves some hygienic purposes – your real hair, which attracts head lice, can be shaved, and your wig is far more easily deloused than your original barnet.

• SELECT A TOP HAT •

A creation of the late eighteenth century, the top hat (also known as the beaver hat, high hat, silk hat, cylinder hat and chimney pot hat) is essential for finishing off that dapper outfit. With many people wearing them by our Victorian age (policemen, for example, wear an oilskin-capped variety), you have to distinguish your hat from that of the masses via quality of fabric – felted beaver fur is always a sign of bearing, although in recent years, and certainly since Prince Albert has donned one, the fashionable preference has been for the silk plush top hat, made from cheesecloth, linen, flannel and shellac. (The shift to this type of hat has had a severe impact on the beaver-trapping industry in Canada.) The classic Empire top hat sits nobly around the forehead and skull, boasting a 2½ to 3in-wide cloth hatband, an authoritative height (up to 8in) and a deep lustre (the shine is by virtue of the shellac being 'baked' into the linen). For occasions of mourning, fit the hat with a deep black band, accented with silk buttons. By contrast, for the opera one might want a collapsible stretched black satin variety, which can be compressed and placed beneath your seat for the show. One thing's for sure – don't be caught out on the street without your hat, and your dignity.

Also from The History Press

BLOODY BRITISH HISTORY

Britain has centuries of incredible history to draw on – everything from Boudica and the Black Death to the Blitz. This local series, harking back to the extraordinary pulp magazines of days gone by, contains only the darkest and most dreadful events in your area's history. So embrace the nastier side of British history with these tales of riots and executions, battles and sieges, murders and regicides, witches and ghosts, death, devilry and destruction!